MW01565082

GEORGIA
GRILLE

^^^^^^^^^^^^^^^^^^^^^

Published in USA by Montgomery Publishing Company, Atlanta, Georgia
Copyright © 2014 Montgomery Publishing Company
Recipes and Text Copyright © 2014 Karen Hilliard
Project Direction, Art Direction and Design: Holly Fisher, Atlanta

Excerpts from Teaching Billy to Cook are from the following:
Copyright © 1994 Montgomery Publishing Company
Recipes and Text copyright © 1994 Karen Hilliard
Georgia Grill Drawings Copyright © 1994 John Ehrlichman
Photographs Copyright © 1994 Lana "Lulu" Lanier
Recipe Editing and Testing: Susan Mack, Cutting Edge Enterprises

Project Direction, Art Direction and Design: Anderson/Griffin, Atlanta

^^^^^^^^^^^^^^^^^^^^

ISBN 978-0-692-30972-8

TEACHING BILLY
TO COOK

25th Anniversary Edition

BY KAREN HILLIARD

THE BEGINNING

I returned to Atlanta from Texas in 1990 and opened Georgia Grille. With no way to see into the future I just worked every day to make the restaurant the best it could be. Here we are celebrating 25 years of food and service and the inevitable question is "where has the time gone". Though certainly not easy, each day has been a blessing. I say thank you to my loyal staff and customers for all the support and encouragement they have given Georgia Grille. A very special thank you to my sweet daughter, Jennifer, her husband Jim and my two fabulous grandsons, Sam and Jack, for giving me their love and understanding when I was "missing in action". And, of course, to Billy-he is my hero.

I know in my heart that God has chosen a path for each of us, how thankful I am for His guidance and love.

Karen Hilliard

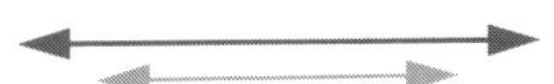

Billy

TABLE OF CONTENTS

= 47 =
DRESSING, MARINADE, SALSA, SAUCE & STOCK

Bacon Buttermilk Dressing 47 • Caesar Dressing 48 • Chile Relleno 49
Habanera Mint Sauce 51 • Jalapeno Tomato Salsa 51
Papaya-Mango Salsa 52 • Pork Chop Brine 52 • Queso 53
Red Chile Jus 53 • Red Chile Sauce 54 • Remoulade Sauce 54
Roasted Corn Salsa 55 • Salmon Marinade 57 • Shrimp Stock 57
Texas BBQ Sauce 58 • Tomatillo-Serrano Chile Sauce 59
Vinaigrette 60 • White Bean Salsa 61

= 65 =
PERFECT PLATES

= 65 =
PORK TENDERLOIN FAJITAS
Apple Chili Chutney 67 • Fried Collard Greens 67

= 69 =
GRILLED SALMON QUESADILLA
Chipotle Cream Sauce 71 • Squash Salsa 71

= 72 =
SHRIMP AND SCALLOPS
Tomato, Red Pepper and Garlic Sauce 73 • Black Pepper Spice Rub 72

= 75 =
HICKORY GRILLED TENDERLOIN
Ripe Tomato Relish 76 • Fried Onion Rings 77

= 78 =
VEGETABLE BURRITO
Smoked Tomato Drizzle 79

= 81 =
NEW PLATES
∧∧∧∧∧∧∧∧∧∧∧∧∧∧∧∧∧∧

Catfish 82 • Jalapeno Cole Slaw 83 • Crayfish Enchilada 84
Fish Tacos 85 • Lamb Tenderloin Quesadilla 87
Navajo Taco 88 • Indian Fry Bread 88 • Shrimp Enchilada 89
Green Chile Quiche 91

= 93 =
A FAVORITE LIBATION
∧∧∧∧∧∧∧∧∧∧∧∧∧∧∧∧∧∧

Dan's Margarita 93

= 95 =
SOMETHING SWEET
∧∧∧∧∧∧∧∧∧∧∧∧∧∧∧∧∧∧

Banana Cheesecake Flauta 97 • Blackberry Peach Cobbler 98
Bread Pudding 99 • Cocoa Mocha Ice Cream Pie 101 • Ganache 102
Glazed Blueberry Cake 103 • Gran Marnier Flan 104
Triple Chocolate Mousse 105 • Vanilla Pouring Cream 106

OUR GEORGIA GRILL FAMILY
∧∧∧∧∧∧∧∧∧∧∧∧∧∧∧∧

Karen i, 62, 94, 107 • Billy ii, vi • Brandon 20, 62, 80, 96,
Barry 32 • Gregory 38 • Carlos 44 • Miguel 50 • Eric 56, 62, 96
Mark 68 • Shine 74 • Pete 86 • Erin 90 • Beth 90
Booty 62, 92, 96 • Ron 100 • David 100 • Tyron 100

Billy

BILLY'S FIRST LESSON

In many ways, Georgia Grille came into the world the same way I did – with little fanfare in a small neighborhood on Atlanta's Peachtree Road. The path that led from the nursery of Crawford Long Hospital to Georgia Grille is a journey of discovery … about myself, about life, about home and, most of all, about my son, Billy.

As I was perfecting my culinary skills in Atlanta, Chicago, New Orleans, West Texas, New Mexico, and France, I did not suspect that the path would bring me back to where it all began. Looking back at all the gaining and losing, marriage, children, and other cooking enterprises, I can't imagine it happening any other way. I brought only the essentials with me in 1990 when I left West Texas: an old Coca-Cola cooler, an equally aged pizza oven, a lot of memories, and many dreams. As I made my home once again in Atlanta, the

cooler and the oven found an honored place at Georgia Grille. In many ways our journey was just beginning then. Ahead, the challenge of teaching Billy to cook would become the most important and necessary part of our success.

The recipes in this cookbook have all been served at one time or another at Georgia Grille, where Southwestern, Cowboy, Indian, Mexican and California flavors abound. Some recipes, like our Creamed Corn Salsa and our Black Beans, have become the building blocks for other recipes. They reflect classical technique and creative preparation. Southwestern flavors have been adapted to traditional "comfort foods," becoming favorites of our customers, of Billy and of mine.

CHICKEN MONTEREY

*Chicken Monterey was my first adventure into Southwestern cooking.
I often prepared the classical "chicken cordon bleu" stuffing a chicken breast
with ham and gruyere cheese. It was a natural move to use green chilies and
Monterey Jack cheese.*

6 double boneless chicken breasts, approx. 6 oz. each
1 teaspoon salt
1-1/2 teaspoons *Mexican Spice Rub,* (page 4)
6 whole fresh green Anaheim chilies, roasted, peeled and
 seeded (see *Smoking & Roasting* page 29). You may
 substitute canned chilies.
12 ounces Monterey Jack cheese, grated
1 cup *Seasoned Flour* (page 5)
2 large eggs, beaten until foamy
2 cups cracker crumbs, medium grind is preferable *(Panko is now
available and is a worthy substitute)*
1/4 cup oil or clarified butter (see *Notes to Billy*)
1/2 cup homemade chicken stock or de-fatted canned broth

Place chicken breasts between two pieces of plastic wrap. Flatten
with a mallet, rolling pin or with the palm of your hand. Sprinkle
inside each double breast with salt and *Mexican Spice Rub*. Top with
1 whole chili, then the grated cheese. Fold each breast in half
covering the cheese-and-chili stuffing. Each should look like a fat
single breast. ✪ Dredge each breast in seasoned flour, dip in the
beaten egg, making sure the egg coats the breast completely. Roll
each breast in cracker crumbs. ✪ Preheat the oven to 375° F. ✪
Heat oil until sizzling in a large skillet with an oven-proof handle.
Add the breasts, being careful not to overcrowd the skillet. Turn
breasts and brown on each side, about 2 minutes. Add chicken stock
to the skillet with the breasts. Cover loosely with foil and place

> ### Notes to Billy:
>
> *1. Diet permitting, brown the chicken breasts in clarified butter. To make clarified butter: melt 2 sticks of unsalted butter in a small skillet over low heat. Pour into a bowl and refrigerate to make it easier to remove congealed clarified butter from the milky substance. The congealed butter, (called ghee in Indian recipes), will not burn at high cooking temperatures like un-clarified butter.*
>
> *2. Beware Salmonella! Be sure you sanitize your utensils, paying special attention to knives and cutting boards. Bacteria is destroyed by heat but can be transmitted to other foods if you use the same knives and cutting boards without washing.*
>
> *3. I prefer medium grind cracker crumbs. If unavailable, use fresh bread crumbs or cornmeal, although the breasts will look different and have a slightly different taste and texture.*

skillet in the oven and bake for 25 to 30 minutes or until the juices are clear when pricked. Serve with *Black Beans* (page 5), *Creamed Corn Salsa* (page 9), and *Fresh Tomato Salsa* (page 11). ✪ Yield: 6 servings.

MEXICAN SPICE RUB

2 tablespoons onion powder
2 tablespoons garlic powder
2 tablespoons paprika
2 teaspoons cayenne pepper
2 teaspoons ground cumin

> ### Notes to Billy:
> *Increase proportionally the ingredients and make a large batch. The mixture will keep fresh for several months.*

Mix together spices. Store in an airtight jar. ✪ Yield: about 1/2 cup.

SEASONED FLOUR

1 cup all purpose flour
1 teaspoon Kosher salt
1/2 teaspoon black pepper

Stir ingredients together. ✪ Yields: about 1 cup. ✪ Ingredient Note: Kosher salt is more coarse than table salt and decreases the danger of over-salting, which is more difficult to correct than under-salting.

NOTES TO BILLY: When you have finished dredging the chicken in the flour, discard what is left because it has been contaminated by the raw chicken.

GEORGIA GRILLE
BLACK BEANS

2 cups dried black beans
  (see directions on page 6 for soaking, if desired)
water to cover beans
3 slices bacon
1 cup onions, dices (about 1 medium)
1 tablespoon garlic, minced (about 2 cloves)
1 tablespoon cilantro leaves, chopped
1 tablespoon salt
1-1/2 teaspoons *Pickled Jalapeño Puree* (see note page 41)
1 teaspoon ground cumin
3 tablespoons *Roasted Spice Rub* (page 7)

In a heavy saucepan or large Dutch oven, cook the black beans covered with water on medium high for about 2-1/4 hours until tender. Make sure that beans stay covered with water during cooking.

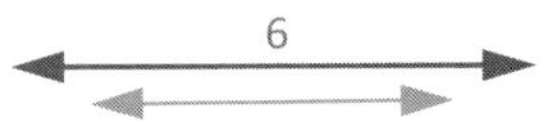

Drain the beans in a colander, rinse with water, then return them to their original cooking pot. Add enough fresh water to barely cover beans again. ✪ In a skillet, cook the bacon until crisp. Drain bacon well, then dice finely and add to bean pot. Remove half the bacon grease from the skillet. Add the onions and the garlic and sauté until

NOTES TO BILLY:
1. If you plan ahead and soak the black beans overnight, the cooking time will be about 50 to 60 minutes.
2. When you drain the cooked black beans, you lose some of the nutrients, but this makes the beans easier on the tummy.
3. For a vegetarian dish you may eliminate the bacon, though you will lose flavor.

translucent. Transfer the onions-garlic mixture to the bean pot with a slotted spoon to leave any remaining bacon grease behind. ✪ Add the cilantro, salt, pickled jalapeño puree and the cumin to the bean pot. ✪ In a dry, non-stick or well seasoned heavy skillet, toast the *Roasted Spice Rub* over medium heat. Do not burn. Add the toasted spices to the beans. ✪ Cook beans for about 40 to 45 minutes more to thicken into a bit of a sauce. Taste for salt. ✪ Yield: six 1 cup servings.

ROASTED SPICE RUB

2 tablespoons ground
cumin
2 tablespoons
oregano (Mexican
leaf oregano is
preferable)
4 teaspoons paprika
2 teaspoons cayenne

Mix all the spices together.
Store in an airtight jar. ✪
Yield: 1/4 cup.

> NOTES TO BILLY:
> To toast the spices, put the amount you need in a dry, non-stick skillet. Do not go off and leave the spices to heat. Cook over medium high heat, stir constantly to prevent burning, about 3 minutes. They will begin to smoke just before they begin to burn. The aroma is wonderful if you do not burn them.

BLACK BEAN SOUP

It might be possible to create a whole restaurant menu using just black beans. They really combine well....sometimes dominating the flavors of the recipe and other times acting as a carrier for other ingredients flavors.

6 cups *Georgia Grille Black Beans* (page 5)
3 cups chicken or vegctable stock or water
1/2 cup *Fresh Tomato Salsa* (page 11)
3 ounces Monterey Jack cheese, grated for garnish

Puree the black beans in the food processor. In a large heavy saucepan or Dutch oven, warm the pureed black beans and the stock over low heat until hot. Garnish with a spoonful of *Fresh Tomato Salsa* and grated Monterey Jack cheese. ✪ If you prefer your soup thicker, add more beans; thinner, add more stock. ✪ Yield: six 2-cup servings.

BLACK BEAN HOLLANDAISE

*If you are lucky enough to get fresh King Salmon from the Pacific,
grill the salmon until lightly cooked over hickory
and serve it with the black bean hollandaise. Heaven!!*

2 egg yolks
3 tablespoons lemon juice
pinch salt
pinch cayenne
dash Tabasco
1 cup (2 sticks) unsalted butter, melted
1/4 cup *Georgia Grille Black Beans* (page 5)

Place yolks, lemon juice, salt, cayenne, Tabasco in food processor. While machine is running, slowly pour in melted butter (still warm). Turn off processor. ✪ Add black beans and puree to desired consistency. I like it a little lumpy. It is especially wonderful if a piece of bacon from the beans is included. Taste for salt. ✪ Yield: six 1/4 cup servings. ✪ You can also use a can of drained black beans for a fast version of this dish.

NOTES TO BILLY:

If you are concerned about the uncooked eggs in the hollandaise, you can use pasteurized eggs with no adjustments in this recipe.

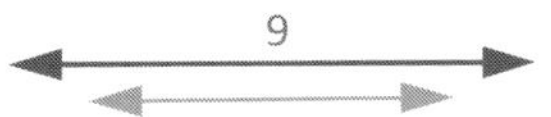

CREAMED CORN SALSA

1 two-pound package frozen corn
2 teaspoons Kosher salt
water
1/4 cup green onions, diced (about 2)
1 tablespoon large shallots, diced (about 2)
1 cup heavy cream
1/4 cup *Roasted Garlic Butter* (page 10)
1/2 cup *Fresh Tomato Salsa*, drained (page 11)
1-1/2 teaspoons Chipotle in Adobe, pureed

Boil the frozen corn in salted water following the package directions. Drain. ✪ Return 2/3 of the corn to the cooking pot and add the onions and shallots. Add the heavy cream. Bring to a boil, then simmer for 5 minutes, stirring often. The cream will reduce slightly and the sauce will thicken. Remove from the heat. ✪ In a food processor, puree the remaining corn and the *Roasted Garlic Butter* until smooth. Add to the corn in the pot. ✪ Stir the tomato salsa and the chipotle pepper in the corn. Reheat slowly if necessary. ✪ Yield: seven 1-cup servings.

NOTES TO BILLY:
This recipe is a take-off on Southern creamed corn. You may certainly use fresh corn; however, the consistency and the efficiency of the frozen corn is a plus. Once you have the Roasted Garlic Butter and the Fresh Tomato Salsa on hand, it is easy to prepare.

ROASTED GARLIC BUTTER

This is a great addition to the Creamed Corn Salsa *and
the* Shrimp and Scallop Sauce, *as well as
a terrific spread on warm bread.*

NOTES TO BILLY:
*Garlic butter is
something you have to
taste in order to
determine how much
garlic should be used.*

1 whole unpeeled garlic bulb
1 pound unsalted butter, softened
salt

Preheat oven to 350°. Wrap garlic in foil.
Roast in the oven for 30 to 45 minutes
until soft. Remove foil. Slice off the
stem end and press to remove pulp. In
the food processor, puree the garlic pulp,
the butter, then salt to taste. ✪ Cover in plastic wrap and store in the
freezer until uses.

GUACAMOLE

4 large avocados peeled, pitted, mashed (preferably by hand)
1-1/2 cups tomatoes, seeded and diced (about 2 large)
1 cup onion, diced, (about 1 medium)
1 tablespoon fresh cilantro, chopped
1 tablespoon lemon juice
2 cloves garlic, minced
2 teaspoons salt or to taste
1 teaspoon pickled jalapeño, pureed (see page 41)
1/2 teaspoon black pepper

Stir all the ingredients together. ✪ *(Note: To slow discoloration during storage, place the avocado pit in the middle of the bowl and seal tightly with plastic wrap, pressing plastic against the guacamole. Refrigerate.)* ✪ Yield: 8 generous 1/2-cup servings; 4-1/2 cups total.

FRESH TOMATO SALSA

This salsa is wonderful to have on hand.
This recipe makes a lot, purposefully, so you will have plenty. However, you can halve all the ingredients to make less. The use of whole cilantro leaves makes it easy for anyone not crazy about its taste to remove it from the salsa.

1-1/2 cups onion, diced (about
   1 large)
3 tablespoons garlic minced
   (about 6 large cloves)
1 tablespoon oil
4 cups tomatoes, seeded and
   diced (about 5 large)
1 ten-ounce can Rotel diced
   tomatoes and green chilies
1/2 cup green onions, sliced
   (about 4)
1/4 cup balsamic vinegar
2 tablespoons rice vinegar
1 tablespoon salt
1/2 teaspoon ground coriander
1/2 teaspoon ground cumin
fresh cilantro leaves for garnish,
   optional

NOTES TO BILLY:
1. It is not mandatory to sauté the onions and garlic. However, if you do, the salsa has a sweeter taste, and the salsa tastes fresher for a longer time.
2. This is a perfect diet dressing: to further minimize fat, either do not sauté the onions and the garlic, or omit the oil. Use a non-stick skillet and cooking spray when you sauté.

Sauté the onions and the garlic in the oil in a large skillet over medium high heat until the onions are soft and translucent. In a large bowl mix all the remaining ingredients except the cilantro. Stir in the garlic-onion mixture. ✪ Garnish the salsa with whole cilantro leaves. ✪ Yield: 2 quarts or sixteen 1/2-cup servings.

GAZPACHO

3 cups *Fresh Tomato Salsa* (page 11)
1-1/2 cups cucumber, peeled, seeded, and diced (about 1 large)
3 Anaheim green chilies, roasted, peeled, seeded and diced
1 medium red bell pepper, smoked, peeled, seeded and diced
1 tablespoon lemon juice
4 dashes Tabasco
4 cups tomato juice
1-1/2 teaspoons salt
1 avocado, diced, garnish
1/2 cup sour cream, garnish
1/4 cup cilantro leaves, garnish

Place *Fresh Tomato Salsa*, cucumber, green chilies, red pepper, lemon juice and Tabasco in the bowl of a food processor. Pulse three times. ✪ Add tomato juice and salt. Pulse once. Do not puree. This is best served chunky. ✪ Chill and serve garnished with avocado, sour cream, and cilantro leaves. ✪ Yield: 6 one-and-a-half cup servings.

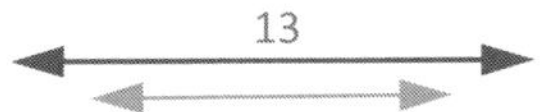

SHALLOT AND GARLIC MASHED POTATOES

5 large potatoes, peeled and chopped
water to cover potatoes
1 tablespoon salt
1 cup heavy cream
1 cup milk
2 cloves garlic, minced
1 large shallot, minced
1 teaspoon white vinegar
2 ounces butter (1/2 stick)
white pepper to taste

Notes to Billy:
1. Until you are familiar with the recipe you might reserve some of the hot milk mixture to add after you check the consistency. Consistency may seem too thin but it will thicken as it sits.
2. Two cups of half-and-half may be substituted for the cream and the milk.

Place potatoes in large saucepan and cover with cold water. Add salt and bring to boil. Reduce heat and simmer until potatoes are tender but firm, not mushy. Dice the potatoes evenly so they cook to the same consistency. When the potatoes are almost cooked, simmer cream, milk, garlic and shallots in another small saucepan for five minutes. ✪ Drain potatoes and place them in large mixing bowl. Immediately pour in hot milk mixture. Add vinegar and butter. Add a pinch of white pepper. Adjust salt and seasonings. ✪ Mix only to combine. Do not over beat; a few lumps are okay. ✪ Yield: 8 generous servings.

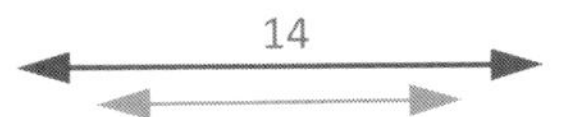

CRUMB CRUST CHICKEN BREAST

The simplicity and comfort of mashed potatoes, lightly blanched julienned carrots, and a crisp cooked chicken breast combine to be the all time - best selling menu item at Georgia Grille.

Mix together approximately 2 cups bread crumbs (optional: substitute Panko), 1 tablespoon chopped parsley, 1 tablespoon pureed garlic and salt to taste. Use a boneless chicken breast for each plate, brush with melted butter or oil, coat well with crumbs, and sauté in oil.

POTATO FRITTERS

This recipe happened because we had leftover mashed potatoes every night when we first opened Georgia Grille. Now we prepare extra potatoes for the fritters.

2 cups *Shallot and Garlic Mashed Potatoes* (page 13)
1 egg, beaten
1/4 cup green onions, diced, (about 2)
1/3 cup onion, diced, (about 1/2 medium)
1 small garlic clove, minced
3 tablespoons parsley, chopped
1/2 cup all-purpose flour
3 tablespoons yellow cornmeal
2 teaspoons salt
2 teaspoons sugar
2 teaspoons baking powder
1 teaspoon ground coriander
1/8 teaspoon cayenne
1/8 teaspoon black pepper
oil for frying

In a large mixing bowl, combine mashed potatoes, egg, green onions, onion, garlic and parsley. Mix well. ✪ In a separate small bowl, mix together flour, cornmeal, salt, sugar, baking powder, coriander, cayenne and black pepper, and stir vigorously into the potato mixture. ✪ In heaping tablespoons full, drop into 360° F. oil. Turn to brown evenly on both sides approximately every 2 to 3 minutes. ✪ The batter may be stored in the refrigerator overnight. Stir well before using. ✪ Yield: eight 4 fritter servings; about 30 fritters total.

HORSERADISH SAUCE

This sauce is a great dipper for the Potato Burritos or Potato Fritters. Also, you can spread it on bread for a pork fajita sandwich or on a tortilla for either chicken or pork fajitas.

1 cup mayonnaise
1/2 cup sour cream
1/4 cup rice vinegar
1 tablespoon Dijon mustard
1-1/2 teaspoons sugar
2 tablespoons horseradish
2 drops Tabasco
cilantro leaves, garnish

Combine ingredients to a smooth consistency. Garnish with cilantro. ✪ Yield: one and three quarters cups. ✪ *(Note: to slim down the horseradish sauce, you can use low-fat mayonnaise and non-fat sour cream or yogurt.)*

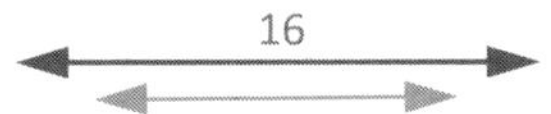

POTATO BURRITO

For best results, you need to fry these immediately after making them.

1 cup chicken stock
8 six-inch white corn tortillas
1 cup uncooked *Potato Fritter* mixture (page 14)
oil for frying
1/2 cup sour cream
1 cup *Green Chili Sauce* (page 17)
Twigs garnish (below)

In a small skillet heat chicken stock. Dip tortilla into the warm stock and place on flat surface. Place approximately 2 tablespoons of fritter mixture on one side of tortilla. Roll up tortilla with the grain. Secure with a toothpick. ✪ Heat oil to 360°. Drop filled tortillas into 3 to 4 inches of hot fat and fry about 3 minutes until lightly browned with the filling cooked through. ✪ Remove toothpick. Place a small dollop of sour cream on plate. Place burrito on top. (This will keep the burrito from flying off the plate and tastes great, too.) ✪ Top with 2 tablespoons *Green Chili Sauce* and a few *Twigs*. ✪ Yield: 8 burritos.

TWIGS

*Blue Corn Tortillas cut in thin strips and deep fried in oil heated to 360°.
You may cut them with a knife or scissors. We cut them with the
noodle cutter on the pasta machine. They add crunch and a
special signature to our presentation at Georgia Grille.*

GREEN CHILI SAUCE

With all the recent interest in Southwestern food, soon it will be easier and more practical to buy a ready-made sauce, especially if you can find one using New Mexico Green Chilies. However, I began making my own sauce the first day we opened Georgia Grille. I order my New Mexico Green Chilies directly from Josie's in Santa Fe, New Mexico by the 50-pound case!! The New Mexico Green Chili is the best fresh chili for this sauce.

1/4 cup onion, diced (about 1/2 small)
2 teaspoons oil
1 teaspoon garlic, pureed (about 1 clove)
2 tablespoons flour
1/2 teaspoon cumin
1/8 teaspoon dried Mexican oregano
6 New Mexico green chilies, roasted, peeled, seeded and diced
      (about 2 cups)
1 cup water or chicken stock
salt to taste

(Note: 3/4 pound of unprepared chilies makes 2 cups prepared.) ✪
Sauté onions in oil until translucent. Stir in garlic and cook one more minute. Stir in flour, cumin and oregano and cook one minute. Add green chilies with accumulated liquid and water or stock. Stir to make a medium thick sauce. Simmer gently for 5 minutes. Thin with additional water or stock to desired consistency. Salt to taste. ✪
Yield: 3 cups.

HONEY WHOLE WHEAT BREAD

4 cups lukewarm water
¾ cups honey
3 tablespoons vegetable oil
3 tablespoons salt
¾ cups powdered non-fat dry milk
3 tablespoons dry yeast
5 cups whole wheat flour
5-6 cups white flour

Preheat oven to 400 degrees. Lightly grease sheet pan. ✷ In large mixer (Kitchen Aid table top), combine water, honey, oil, salt and powdered milk. Add yeast and proof for 10 minutes. ✷ Mix in whole wheat flour. Mix well and add white flour a little at a time until dough is smooth and elastic. The dough will begin to pull away from the sides. Let the dough rise until it doubles in size. Punch down and let it rise until it doubles again. Punch down a second time. After second rise remove dough from bowl and place on a lightly floured surface. ✷ Divide bread in fourths. Shape in loaves and place on a lightly greased sheet pan. Let dough rise again. Mark bread with a knife and spray with water. ✷ Bake in 400 degree oven for 12 minutes. ✷ Turn pans (rotate 180 degrees) and bake for another 12 minutes. ✷ Yield: 4 small loaves

CHEESE QUESADILLA

6" Flour Tortillas

Cheese Stuffing:
    1 cup Monterrey Jack cheese, shredded
    ½ cup white cheddar cheese, Shredded
    ½ cup parmesan cheese, Grated
    ¼ cup mayonnaise

Combine all ingredients and mix well. ✶ Spread 1/2 cup stuffing on one 6" tortilla. Top with another tortilla. Place on dry flat grill or in a black iron skillet. Over medium heat cook, turning once, until both sides are lightly browned and cheese melted. Cut in half twice (four pieces).

Great appetizer or light meal at Georgia Grille. We serve with a small side of guacamole and fresh tomato salsa. Make it a Chicken Quesadilla with grilled chicken slices.

Left over tortillas may be frozen. Store stuffing, covered in the refrigerator.

Brandon

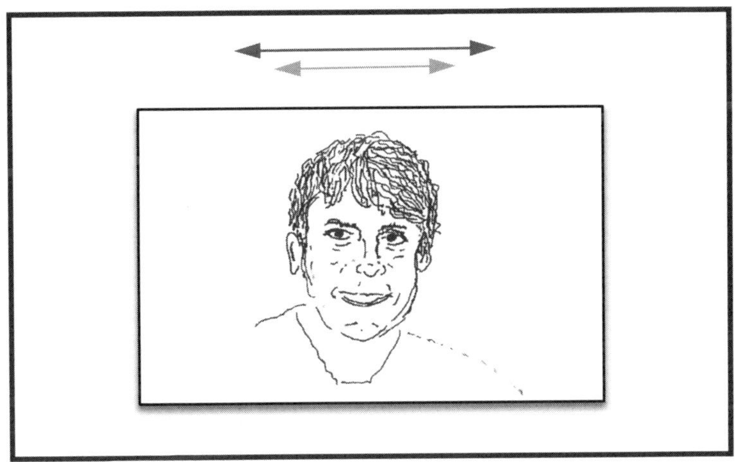

BILLY ON HIS OWN

"Where did you study cooking?" a customer once asked Billy. He replied, "My mother taught me and I had to get it right the first time." Admittedly, during Billy's early years, there was never a plan that he follow me into the restaurant business. I didn't own my first restaurant until he was in

college. The idea of a son going into business with his father is traditional. Perhaps in today's world it is becoming the norm for sons and daughters to follow in their mother's footsteps! What a great compliment it is to me. Teaching Billy to cook was only the beginning. He has now learned how to work productively with his employees, and he knows the significance of entrepreneurial decisions. I see his concern for customers. And, (though these may not be found in any textbook), he has also acquired a knack for keeping his mother happy and coping with very little sleep!

The proper ending is no ending...it all continues. More teaching and learning, more great food and friends. The path Billy chooses is his own. he's on his way.

SERRANO CHILI OIL

Brush this oil on meats, vegetables and seafood before grilling. Use a good quality olive oil for this recipe, though extra-virgin is not necessary.

    2 cups olive oil
    1 cup fresh Serrano chilies, whole

In a deep covered heavy pan, bring the oil and the chilies to a boil. Reduce heat and simmer 15 minutes. Cool mixture. Drain the chilies from the oil. Store the oil in the refrigerator. ✪ The chilies may be added to salsas. ✪ Yield: 2 cups.

BLACK BEAN AND CUMIN PANCAKE
WITH GRILLED SHRIMP
AND POBLANO SAUCE

*This is a special occasion appetizer.
It takes a bit of time, but it is wonderful.*

Pancake:
    1-1/4 cups milk
    1 cup flour
    2 *eggs*, beaten
    2 teaspoons salt
    1-1/2 teaspoons cayenne
    1-1/2 teaspoons cumin
    1-1/4 cups *Georgia Grille Black Beans*, pureed, (page 5)
        (Note: drained canned black beans can be substituted)
    1/4 cup melted, clarified butter or oil (page 4, note)

Whisk together eggs, flour, milk, salt, cumin and cayenne. Stir black beans and butter into milk mixture. Refrigerate for one hour. ✪ Heat a small skillet and add a drizzle of oil. Pour three tablespoons of pancake batter into hot skillet. Cook until bubbles appear. Turn and cook for one minute. Remove completed pancakes to a plate in a 100° to 125° oven. Cover with a terry-cloth towel.

GRILLED SHRIMP

18 large shrimp, peel and butterfly
1/4 cup *Serrano Chili Oil* (page 23)
1/4 cup *Mexican Spice Rub* (page 4)
salt

Brush shrimp with *Serrano Chili Oil*. Sprinkle with salt and *Mexican Spice Rub*. Grill about 2 to 3 minutes over wood, turning until cooked pink.

Assembly:
6 full size pancakes
18 cooked shrimp
1 cup *Smoked Poblano Cream* (page 42)
Twigs (page 16)garnish optional

Presentation:
Place pancake on plate, top with three shrimp, drizzle sauce over shrimp and pancake. Garnish with *Twigs*. ✪ Yield: 6 appetizer portions.

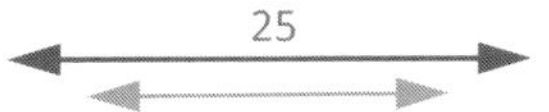

BILLY'S BOURBON PEACH CHUTNEY

Great with hickory grilled Pork Chops!!!!

1 teaspoon garlic clove, minced (about 1 small)
1 teaspoon shallot, minced (about 1 small)
1/2 teaspoon jalapeño, minced
2 teaspoons oil
3/4 cup water
1 cup apple cider vinegar
1/2 cup granulated sugar
1/2 cup dark brown sugar
5 fresh peaches, peeled, pitted and diced (about 2-1/2 cups)
(Note: frozen may be substituted)
8 whole cloves
1/2 teaspoon red chili powder
1/2 teaspoon dry mustard powder (ground mustard)
3/4 cup bourbon

Sauté the garlic, shallots and jalapeños in the oil for about 1 minute in a non-reactive, large saucepan. ✪ Stir in the water, vinegar and the sugars and bring to a boil over high heat. Stir occasionally. ✪ Reduce the heat to medium and add the peaches, cloves, chili powder and dry mustard. Cook for about 20 to 25 minutes until very thick and chunky. ✪ Remove from heat and stir in bourbon. Puree in the food processor, or if you prefer, leave chunky. Serve warm with grilled meats or chicken. ✪ Yield: eight 1/2-cup servings.

PORK CHOP

This chutney is wonderful with a hickory grilled pork chop. I suggest a center cut, about one inch thick. Brush each side of the chop with some chutney before you place it on the grill. Serve with additional chutney on the plate.

EXPENSIVE MUSHROOM CREAM SAUCE

Billy serves this sauce over a Blue Corn Tortilla, but the sauce is so flavorful it has lots of uses, such as over polenta or veal chop. A fabulous fall dinner is pasta tossed with this mushroom sauce and either tenderloin of beef or venison. Not bad for New Year's Eve, either, with plenty of champagne!!

2 tablespoons garlic, minced (about 2 cloves)
1/4 cup onion, diced (about 1/2 small)
2 tablespoons *Serrano Chili Oil* (page 23)
3 cups shitake or oyster mushrooms, stems removed and sliced
3 cups button mushrooms, sliced
1 cup white wine
2 cups heavy cream
2 tablespoons fresh thyme leaves
1 tablespoon cilantro, chopped
1 tablespoon salt

Cook garlic and onions in the *Serrano Chili Oil* for 2 minutes, over medium, heat until onions are translucent. Add mushrooms and cook until mushrooms are soft. ✪ Add wine, bring to boil. Simmer until the liquid is reduced to 3 tablespoons. Raise heat to high and add cream. Bring to a boil, then reduce heat and simmer for 12 to 15 minutes. Remove from heat and add thyme, cilantro and salt. ✪ Yield: eight 1/2-cup servings; 4 cups total.

PEPPERS, SMOKING AND ROASTING

As with life, a restaurant is about growth and change. Both are built upon layers of experience, taste, and people. The unique flavors at Georgia Grille are the result of blending those layers.

We began by using hickory chips and then we were able to buy a new grill that used split hickory logs. The sensual aroma alone makes cooking with wood worth the time and effort. What the wood smoke does to food is magic. The depth of taste and flavor that comes from smoking and roasting can be subtle or intense. Either way it is addictive. When I discovered this magic, it opened up a flood of ideas that have

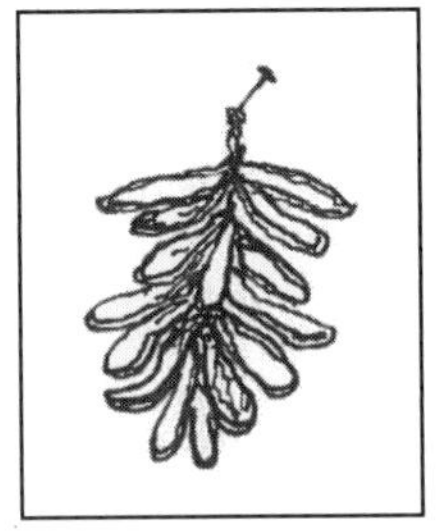

become award winning dishes! At the same time, another kind of magic was going on at Georgia Grille. As the days passed, Billy mastered the basics of cooking and we began to have time to experiment. We gained confidence in each other, in ourselves and in our ability to serve wonderful food to our customers. We finally relaxed, really happy with what we were doing, and our little restaurant became a success.

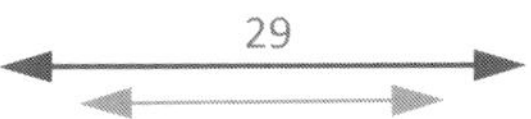

I use Hickory wood on a wood burning open grill for roasting. I cover the whole grill with a lid for smoking. There are advantages to a restaurant kitchen with an adequate ventilation system and large professional equipment. With a smoker or home outdoor grill, however, you should be able to accomplish nearly similar results. Create a fire according to manufacturer's directions.

PEPPER VARIETIES
FOR SMOKING AND ROASTING

ANAHEIM: long green chile, readily available; mildest of the spicy peppers

BELL PEPPERS: all types, especially red

GUERO: light blond in color, flavor gains depth when roasted

HABANERO: color ranges from pale green to bright orange, hottest of the pepper family

JALAPEÑO: bright green, about 2 inches in length, readily available and most widely used pepper in the United States

NEW MEXICO GREEN: similar to the Anaheim, seldom seen in stores outside of New Mexico

NEW MEXICO RED: ripe version of the New Mexico Green; nutty, smoky flavor

POBLANO: a wonderful chili that can be stuffed, diced or pureed to add depth and intensity to an unlimited number of dishes

SERRANO: a small light green chili with intense, pure heat

SMOKING: I suggest smoking large quantities and preserving them under refrigeration or freezing. Make sure peppers are clean and free from major blemishes. Place whole pepper on grill, cover and create a vent for smoke to travel over and through the peppers. Timing is subjective. If you are going to puree the peppers and add to sauces, they will benefit from the longest smoking time. If you are going to dice and want the pepper to have a firmer texture, then smoke for an intermediate time. Depending on your fire and equipment as well as

the texture of the pepper, you will have to allow for trial and error. Remove from grill, cover with a plastic bag, let cool. Using gloves to protect your hands, peel, remove seeds and stem.

ROASTING: Place peppers on open grill over hickory wood fire, turning often to blister entire pepper. Less time spent over the fire will result in a crisper pepper. Remove from grill, cover with a plastic bag, let cool. Using gloves to protect your hands, peel, remove seeds and stem. Roasted peppers will not have as much hickory smoked flavor. However, they will be easier to stuff or use whole for a special plate presentation. Served chilled on a salad plate, as a garnish for the dinner plate, or stuffed whole in a chicken breast.

OTHER FOODS

ROASTING AND SMOKING TOMATOES: Roma tomatoes are the variety of choice. They may be smoked or roasted the same as peppers. Another suggestion: heat a black iron skillet to medium and without any oil or liquid, roast tomatoes until the skins are well charred. This brings out the natural flavors so often missing in commercially grown tomatoes.

CORN: Remove husk and silk from corn and smoke or roast on the cob the same as peppers, being careful not to blacken the kernels extensively. For salsas I prefer to roast the corn kernels, cut off the cob in a heated black iron skillet without oil, letting the natural sugars caramelize to bring out the sweet flavors.

VEGETABLES: Vegetables on the grill are the answer to a vegetarian's dream and a dieter's delight. Brushing them with chili oil or using a spicy rub and cooking them over hickory makes your taste buds think you're eating meat! Take care not to overcook or char past the point of good taste. One of my favorite combinations is the *Roasted Corn Salsa* over grilled sweet potato wedges!!

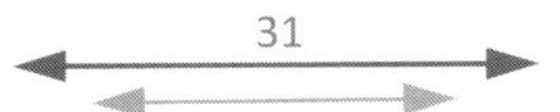

CHEESE JALAPENO GRITS

1 cup stone ground all natural grits
2 ½ cups milk
2 ½ cups water
1 cup Monterey jack cheese
2 tablespoons butter
1 ½ teaspoon salt
1 tablespoons jalapeno, pureed
2 eggs
1 cup heavy cream

Use a Le Cruset (or similar) pot. ⋆ Place grits in pot and cover with water. Stir and then pour off as much water as possible. Stir in 2 ½ cups milk. ⋆ Heat 2 ½ cups water to boiling and pour into grits. Bring to boil and then turn down heat and cook until lightly thickened, 5 – 10 minutes. Stir in cheese, butter, salt and jalapenos. ⋆ Whip the eggs with the heavy cream, temper, and pour slowly, stirring, into grits. ⋆ Bake in 350 degree oven for 20 to 30 minutes.

ROAST PORK

4 pound Boston butt roast (cut in two to three pieces)

Wipe clean and pat dry. Sprinkle with salt and pepper. Using a black iron skillet brown pork on all sides. Remove pork from skillet and place in slow cooker with one cup chicken stock. Cook for 7 hours on low. ⋆ Remove pork to a cutting board. Using a fork, shred the meat. Refrigerate. ⋆ Strain liquid that is left in the slow cooker. Refrigerate. Remove and discard the grease that has solidified. Heat the reserved liquid and toss with pork.

Barry

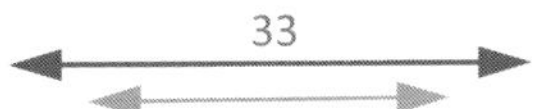

COWBOY ROAST PORK SANDWICH

Per Serving:
    Large flour tortillas
    Pork Roast, shredded (page 31)
    White Bean Salsa (page 61)
    Green Chile Sauce (page 17)
    White Sauce (page 40)
    Monterey Jack Cheese, shredded

Layer the pork, white bean salsa and green chile on a flour tortilla. ✴
Roll and place seam side down on a heat proof plate. Cover the
tortilla with white sauce and top with ¼ cup Monterey Jack cheese. ✴
Bake @350 degrees for 12 minutes (until hot in the center). ✴ Serve
with *Fresh Tomato Salsa* (page 11) and a side of *Texas BBQ Sauce*
(page 58) and *Jalapeno Cole Slaw* (page 83)

*This is rather like any other sandwich…..the amount of the
ingredients is very subjective. The combination of flavors is what it is
all about!*

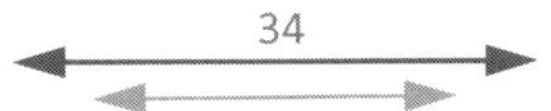

CREOLE GUMBO

1 ¼ cup oil
1 ½ cups flour
6 cups onions, chopped
4 cups Poblano pepper, chopped
3 cups celery, chopped
1 tablespoon garlic, minced
2 teaspoons black pepper
2 teaspoons white pepper
½ teaspoon cayenne
1/8 teaspoon thyme
¼ teaspoon oregano
2 teaspoons salt
6 cups chicken stock
1 ½ pounds Kielbasa sausage, browned and slightly cooked
6 cup hickory smoked chicken, white and dark meat.

Brown sausage, then cover with water and boil until tender. Slice into medium dice. ✶ Heat oil until smoking. Add flour stirring constantly until the roux is the color of coca-cola. Add 1/2 of the vegetables and all the spice and stir until all is coated with the roux. Turn off the heat. ✶ Add the remaining vegetables, stir and add 6 cups chicken stock plus 6 cups water. Bring to a boil. Lower heat and simmer adding sausage and chicken. ✶ Add shrimp to order.

LOBSTER ENCHILADA

This dish won the Georgia Seafood Challenge Governor's Cup. Some customers wouldn't eat anything else at Georgia Grille.

2 tablespoons shallots, diced (about 1 large)
1 tablespoon garlic, pureed (about 2 cloves)
1 tablespoon pickled jalapeño puree (page 30)
1-1/2 teaspoons oil
3 cups chicken stock
2 cups heavy cream
1 pound cooked lobster, diced in large chunks
  (see *Buying Lobster* at the end of recipe)
1-1/2 cups grated Monterey Jack cheese (about 5 ounces)
1 red bell pepper, smoked and diced
  (see *Smoking and Roasting*, page 29)
1 large tomato, diced (about 1 cup)
1 tablespoon cilantro, minced
2 teaspoons lime juice
1/4 teaspoon marjoram
12 eight-inch flour tortillas, softened (page 70, note)
3/4 cup grated Monterey Jack cheese, (about 3 ounces)
1 cup *Fresh Tomato Sal*sa (page 11)

Sauté shallots, garlic and jalapeño in oil over medium high heat. Add chicken stock and reduce by half. Add cream and reduce by half. ✪ Stir in lobster, 1-1/2 cups cheese, pepper, tomato, cilantro, lime juice and marjoram. Do not boil or cheese will separate. Keep the filling warm. ✪ Soften the tortillas. Spoon 1/4 cup of filling into each softened tortilla. Roll into a cylinder. Put the enchilada in an ovenproof pan, seam side down. Pour any leftover lobster sauce over the enchilada. Sprinkle with 3/4 cup of grated cheese. Broil the

enchilada to melt cheese. To serve, top each with 2 tablespoons *Fresh Tomato Salsa.* ✪ Note: Buying lobster: one 3-pound, two 2-pound, or three 1-plus-pound lobsters all yield enough meat in the tail and claws. Or purchase frozen tails which have little waste. The fishmonger can also guide you on the amount of whole lobsters to buy. ✪ Yield: six 2-enchilada entrees; twelve one-enchilada appetizer portions.

PUMPKIN CHOWDER

¼ cup vegetable oil
1 cup onions, small dice
1 tablespoon jalapeño, puree
6 cups potatoes, diced
6 cups chicken stock
2 -15 ounce cans pureed pumpkin
1 cup heavy cream
¼ cup smoked poblano chile peppers, diced
1 teaspoon cumin
1 teaspoon salt

Heat oil in a ceramic type pot.   Add onions, and jalapeño and sauté until translucent. Add diced potatoes, stirring for one minute. Pour in stock and bring to a boil. Cook until potatoes are medium soft. Turn off heat. ✶ Remove 2 cups of potatoes and place in a food processor. Pour cream in the processor and process until smooth. Pour potatoes and cream back into pot and turn heat to medium. Stir in pumpkin. Bring to simmer and stir in peppers and cumin. Salt to taste.

ROASTED CORN SALSA

2 cups fresh corn kernels, cut off the ear
1/2 cup red bell pepper, diced
1/2 cup purple onion - diced (about 1 small)
2 tablespoons rice vinegar
1 tablespoon cilantro, coarsely chopped
1 tablespoon parsley, coarsely chopped
2 teaspoons *Pickled Jalapeño* puree (page 41, note)
2 teaspoons salt
1 teaspoon garlic, pureed
1 teaspoon fresh oregano
1 teaspoon fresh thyme

Roast corn in a well seasoned, black iron skillet to "sizzle" stage, caramelizing natural sugars. Mix well with other ingredients. It is important to taste and correct the quantity of fresh herbs. This is a suggested amount of herbs and it is best to add a little at a time and taste. Flavors will become more intense if you wait a few hours to serve. You could also gently heat before serving. ✪ Yield: 5 half-cup servings; 2-1/2 cups total.

Gregory

SMOKED CHICKEN CHOWDER

We take this off the menu during the summer. Customers moan and groan, but I think it is too heavy for Georgia's muggy summer days. We replace it with Gazpacho that has no fat in it at all. Theoretically, you could say that if you have the chowder in the winter and the Gazpacho in the summer, it cuts the fat and calories by one half. (Good try, Karen!!)

3 double boneless skinless chicken breasts
   (about 6 or 8 ounces each), hot smoked over hickory
2 cups onions, diced (about 2 medium)
1/2 cup oil
3 cloves garlic, minced
1 cup peeled and diced potato, (about 1 large)
1/4 cup all-purpose flour
3 cups chicken stock
2 cups *Creamed Corn Salsa* (page 9)
2 cups heavy cream
2 medium tomatoes, smoked, seeded and diced
   (see *Smoking* page 30)
1 cup grated Monterey Jack cheese (about 4 ounces)
1 tablespoon *Green Chili Sauce* (page 17)
2 teaspoons parsley, chopped
salt to taste

Chop smoked chicken breast into small pieces. Reserve. ✪ Sauté onions in a large saucepan or Dutch oven in oil until translucent. Stir in garlic and potatoes, continue to cook, stirring occasionally to keep potatoes from sticking to pot for about 3 minutes. ✪ Sprinkle flour over potato-onion mixture and cook for 1 minute. Add chicken stock. Stir to mix all the ingredients well, bringing to a boil. ✪ Reduce heat and add *Corn Salsa*, cream, tomatoes, cheese, *Green Chili Sauce*, and parsley. Simmer 5 minutes over low heat. Taste for salt. ✪ Stir in reserved smoked chicken. Add additional chicken stock or water to thin if necessary. ✪ Yield: six 2-cup servings.

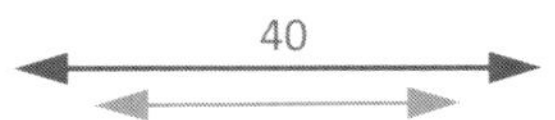

SMOKED CHICKEN ENCHILADA
WITH FRESH TOMATO SALSA

This dish is a great party or potluck dish. It can be prepared in steps in advance and baked at the last minute.

White Sauce:

> 6 tablespoons oil
> 6 tablespoons all-purpose flour
> 4 cups chicken stock
> 3/4 cup green chilies, roasted, peeled, seeded and diced, divided (see *Smoking and Roasting* on page 29)

Heat oil in saucepan until hot. Stir in flour and whisk a few minutes to cook flour. Reduce heat and stir in chicken stock. Stir until sauce is fairly thick. Stir in 1/4 cup green chilies. Makes 4 cups.

Filling:

> 4 double boneless chicken breasts, hickory-smoked until juices are clear
> 1 cup onion, diced (about 1 medium)
> 1-1/2 cups sour cream
> 12 eight-inch white corn tortillas
> 1 cup chicken stock
> 1-1/2 cups Monterey Jack cheese, grated (about 6 ounces)

Preheat oven to 350° F. Dice chicken breasts to 1/2-inch cubes. Mix chicken, 1 cup white sauce, 1 cup onions, the sour cream and remaining 1/2 cup green chilies. ✪ Place 1/3 cup chicken filling on each tortilla. Roll tortillas, then place seam side down on a greased oven-proof dish or sheet pan. Pour remaining white sauce over the enchilada. Sprinkle them with Monterey Jack cheese. Place in oven or under broiler until heated through and cheese melts. ✪

Plate Presentation:
  1 cup *Fresh Tomato Salsa* (page 11)
  1 cup green chile sauce (page 17)
  1/2 cup parsley, chopped
  Twigs garnish optional

Top with 2 tablespoons of *Fresh Tomato Salsa*, parsley, *Twigs* on top.
✪ *(Note: if you used canned chilies rather than fresh, add 1 teaspoon jalapeño puree to
the sauce.)* ✪ Yield: Serves six 2 enchilada entrée portions. ✪
Optional: Serve with *Taco Salad*

NOTES TO BILLY:
Pickled Jalapeño Puree
I prefer to use pickled jalapeños rather than fresh. Puree a jar of them with the juice and store the puree in the refrigerator for quick and easy access.

TACO SALAD

2 cups mayonnaise
1 cup milk
1 tablespoon sugar
1 cup cucumber, peeled, seeded and diced
1 cup tomato, dices
Head lettuce or romaine lettuce chopped small or shredded.

Combine first five ingredients and pour desired amount over lettuce.
✷ We serve in a taco shell with the *Smoked Chicken Enchilada*

SMOKED POBLANO CREAM

2 shallots, minced
3 garlic cloves, minced
2 teaspoons *Pickled Jalapeño*, pureed (page 41, note)
2 teaspoons butter
1 cup chicken stock
1-1/2 cups heavy cream
1/4 cup smoked poblanos, minced
   (see *Smoking Peppers* page 29)
2 tablespoons chopped tomato, garnish (optional)
1 teaspoon chopped parsley, garnish (optional)

Sauté shallots, garlic and jalapeños in butter. Add chicken stock and reduce by half. Add cream and reduce by half. Stir in smoked poblanos. You can stir in chopped tomato and parsley for additional color and flavor. ✪ Yield: eight 1/4-cup servings ✪ Note: serve this with a hickory grilled tuna steak!!

SMOKED TROUT TOSTADO

6 white corn tortillas
oil for frying
1/2 cup rice vinegar
1/2 cup olive oil
2 tablespoons lemon juice
2 tablespoons lime juice
2 cups red bell peppers, seeded,
   julienned thin (about 2)
1/2 cup tomato, seeded, diced, (about 1 small tomato)
1/2 cup purple onion, julienned thin
1/2 cup green onions, green part only thinly sliced (about 4)
1/2 cup fresh basil, julienned
1 teaspoon *Pickled Jalapeño*, pureed (page 41, note)
salt to taste
1/2 cup sour cream
3 fillets of smoked trout, skinned and julienned
1-1/2 cups salad greens
Twigs (page 16)

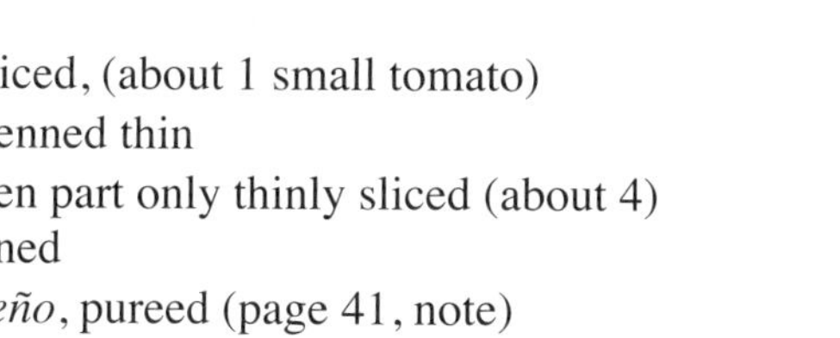

Deep fry the corn tortillas in a bowl shape. Heat oil to 360°. Drop tortilla into the hot oil. Press and hold a large soup ladle into the center of the tortilla to form the bowl shape. When the tortilla is golden, carefully remove it from the oil. Drain well. ✪ Whisk together the vinegar, olive oil, lemon and lime juice. Stir in red bell pepper, tomatoes, onion, green onion, basil, jalapeño and salt to make a salsa. ✪ *To Serve*: Put a dollop of sour cream in the middle of each of six plates. The sour cream acts like glue. Place one deep fried corn tortilla on top of sour cream. Divide the salad greens and trout evenly inside the 6 tortilla bowls. Spoon the salsa evenly on top. Garnish with *Twigs*. ✪ Yield: 6 servings.

Carlos

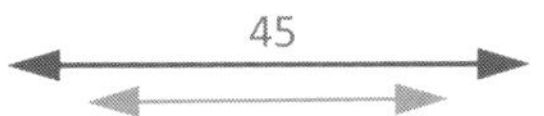

SPICY MACARONI AND CHEESE

¼ cup butter, unsalted
¾ cup onions, small dice
2 teaspoon garlic, minced
3 teaspoon jalapeños, minced
½ teaspoon coriander
¾ teaspoon cumin
2 tablespoon flour, all purpose
1 cup whole milk
1 cup heavy cream
1 ¼ cup tomatoes, small dice
¾ teaspoon salt
½ teaspoon cayenne pepper
½ pound elbow macaroni
¾ teaspoon salt
½ teaspoon cayenne pepper
1 ½ cup Monterey Jack cheese, grated
¾ cup bread crumbs
2/3 cup parmesan cheese, grated
3 tablespoons unsalted butter

In a large skillet or small pot, sauté onions, garlic, jalapenos, coriander and cumin in the butter until the onions arc softened. Stir in flour and cook mixture for 3 minutes, stirring constantly. Combine milk and cream and pour mixture in a stream. Bring to a boil while whisking. Add tomatoes and simmer for 2 minutes. Add salt and cayenne to taste. ✻ In boiling water, cook pasta for 6-7 minutes or until barely al dente. Drain pasta and mix with tomato mixture. Stir in the Monterey Jack cheese. ✻ Transfer to a baking dish. (2 quart Pyrex). ✻ Mix bread crumbs and parmesan cheese, spread evenly over top of mixture. Place unsalted butter over bread crumbs. ✻ Cook for 20-30 minutes in oven at 350 degrees.

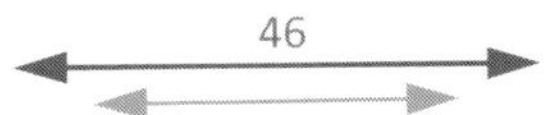

TEXAS CORNBREAD

¾ cup butter

3 cups yellow cornmeal

1-1/2 cups white flour

1-1/2 teaspoon salt

1-1/2 tablespoon baking powder

1-1/2 teaspoon baking soda

1-1/2 cups buttermilk

1-1/2 cups whole milk

3 eggs

3/4 cup butter

3 tablespoon jalapeno, pureed

1-1/2 cups Monterey Jack cheese, grated

Preheat oven to 400 degrees. ✶ Place butter in a 12" iron skillet and put in the oven while mixing corn bread. ✶ Combine dry ingredients in one bowl. ✶ Combine liquid ingredients including jalapeno and cheese in another bowl. ✶ Stir dry and liquid ingredients together. Pour melted butter into mixture and pour all back into the skillet. This will be filled to the top. ✶ Bake @ 400 degrees for about 25-30 minutes. ✶ Let cool for 10 minutes and turn over on to plate or board.

A note about jalapenos: Most of the recipes are made with pickled jalapenos. Pureed and cooked they add a more even heat than fresh jalapenos. When using fresh I suggest that you sear them in a skillet, remove the seed and then puree.

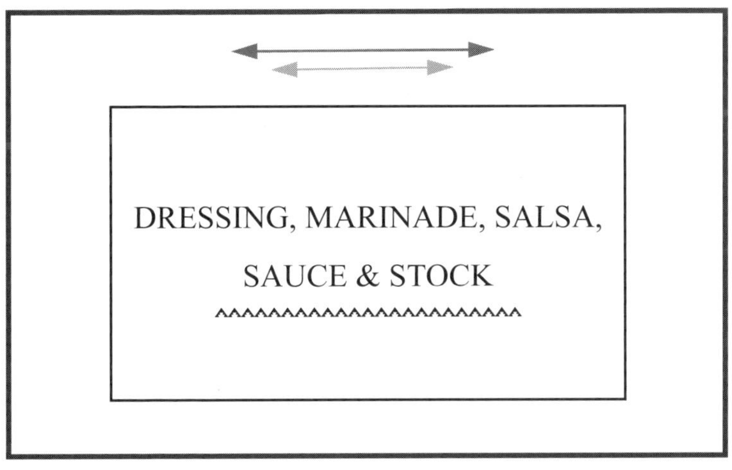

DRESSING, MARINADE, SALSA, SAUCE & STOCK

BACON BUTTERMILK DRESSING

3 cups mayonnaise
1 cup buttermilk
¼ cup green onions, green only, chopped
¼ cup bacon grease
1 pound bacon, cooked crisp, small dice

Dice bacon and cook in skillet until crisp. Remove and drain on paper towel. Reserve ¼ cup of bacon grease. Place on cutting board and dice very small. Place mayonnaise in bowl and whisk in buttermilk. Stir in green onion, bacon grease and cooked bacon.

We use this for a salad dressing or with fried shrimp as a tasty dip.

CAESAR DRESSING

1 1/2 tablespoon garlic, minced
2 tablespoon pureed anchovies
¾ cup parmesan cheese, grated
1 ½ cup olive oil
3 tablespoon lemon juice
2 teaspoon Dijon mustard
1 tablespoon Worcestershire
1/2 teaspoon black pepper, ground
1 teaspoon sugar
1 tablespoon heavy cream

Puree garlic and anchovies in food processor. Add parmesan cheese and pulse to combine. Add the remaining ingredients into processor. PULSE only until mixed. DO NOT OVERMIX. ★ Yield: 2 cups

CHILE RELLENO

6 Anaheim Peppers. Flash fry. Place in ice water. Remove skin. Make a slit in the side.

Cheese Stuffing:
    1 cup Monterrey Jack cheese, shredded
    ½ cup white cheddar cheese, shredded
    ½ cup parmesan cheese, grated
    ¼ cup mayonnaise

Combine all ingredients and mix well. ✶ Fill prepared pepper with cheese mixture (*good idea to use gloves*) The amount may vary depending on the size of the peppers.

For breading:
(I *suggest using 3 small loaf pans for the flour, eggs and panko*)
    2 cups seasoned flour (salt)
    2 whole eggs and a splash of warm water, whipped
    2 cups Japanese bread crumb (panko) (seasoned with salt)
    (The *panko works best if processed to a finer texture*)

Toss stuffed peppers in flour. Dredge with egg mixture. Coat with panko. ✶ Refrigerate.

To serve: Place *Tomatillo Serrano Chile Sauce* (page 59) to cover plate. ✶ Deep fry pepper and place over sauce. See *Frying* (page 82) ✶ Garnish with *Roasted Corn Salsa.*(page 55) ✶ Mark with *Red Chile Jus* (page 53)

50

MIGUEL

HABANERA MINT SAUCE

1 cup fresh mint, minced
¼ cup habanera sauce (bottled)
2 cup mayonnaise
2 cup sour cream
1 cup heavy cream, whipped
¼ cup sugar

Mix together the mint, habanera sauce, mayonnaise and sour cream.
✷ Whip cream and sugar to soft peak and stir in the sugar. Combine
and use as a garnish for meat or fish.

JALAPENO TOMATO SALSA

2 tablespoons jalapenos, minced (page 41, note)
1 ½ tablespoons garlic, minced
3 cups canned or fresh diced tomatoes
> *Note: Works with all canned and pureed tomatoes*
1 cup green onions, chopped
1 ½ tablespoons cumin, ground
1 ½ tablespoons coriander, ground
1 tablespoon salt
2 tablespoons white vinegar
2 tablespoons cilantro, chopped
1 ½ tablespoons sugar

Place jalapeno and garlic in food processor and run to mince well.
Add remaining ingredients and pulse. Taste for seasoning and salt.

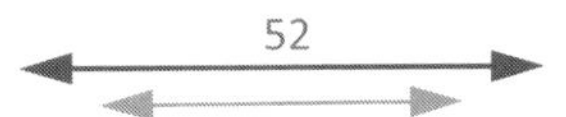

PAPAYA/MANGO SALSA

2 cups fresh papayas, small dice
2 cups fresh mango, small dice
1 cup red bell pepper, small dice
¼ cup green onion, small dice
2 tablespoons fresh cilantro, chopped
¼ cup rice wine vinegar
½ cup purple onions, small dice

Combine all ingredients and refrigerate.

PORK CHOP BRINE
(For grilled Pork Chops)

¼ cup kosher salt
¼ cup granulated sugar
1/3 cup boiling water
5 cups cold water
1 teaspoon black pepper

Place pork chops in a glass container. Pour brine over them making sure they are well submerged. Cover tightly and refrigerate for at least 4 hours. *(Alternately you could use a sealable plastic bag making sure the closure is secure.)*

QUESO

2 ½ cups milk
2 ½ pounds Casa Solano Cheese *(Land O'Lakes white American cheese)*, grated
2 cups Monterey jack cheese, grated
1-10 ounce can Rotel and green chiles, well drained
1 cup green chile sauce (page 17)
2 teaspoons cumin, ground
2 teaspoons garlic, minced
½ cup smoked poblano peppers, seeded and diced

Heat milk and stir in cheeses. Continue to cook over low heat to melt cheese. Stir in remaining ingredients. Mix well. Keep warm at service.

RED CHILE JUS

1 cup Veal demi-glace
1 cup Red Chile Sauce
1 small smoked red bell pepper (pureed)
1 tablespoon honey
Salt to taste

Combine all ingredients and strain.

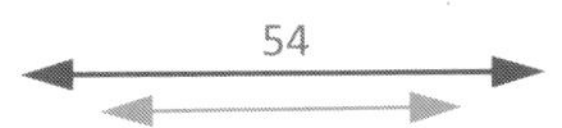

RED CHILE SAUCE

1/4 cup vegetable oil
1/2 cup onions, finely chopped
2 teaspoon garlic, minced
1/2 teaspoon oregano (ground)
½ tablespoon cumin (ground)
1/4 cup flour
1 cup New Mexico red chile powder
5 cups water
1/2 teaspoon salt

Heat oil over medium heat. Add onions and garlic and sauté gently
for about five minutes. ✶ Stir in the oregano, cumin and flour. Cook,
stirring constantly until the mixture is very light brown. ✶ Mix the
chile powder and water until smoothly blended. Pour into flour/onion
paste, stirring to prevent lumps. ✶ Bring the sauce to a boil, being
careful not to scorch. Reduce heat and simmer to desired consistency,
about 30 minutes.

REMOULADE SAUCE

2 cloves garlic
1 small onion
1 cup mayonnaise
½ cup chile sauce (Heinz)
½ cup ketchup
½ cup vegetable oil
1 teaspoon cracked black pepper
dash paprika
dash Tabasco

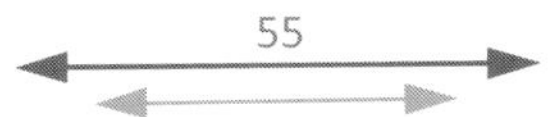

1 tablespoon Worcestershire sauce
1 tablespoon water
1 tablespoon vinegar
1 teaspoon prepared mustard

Mince garlic and onion fine in a processor. Add remaining ingredients. Process until well blended. (You could also use a blender) Possibly add a little more mustard to increase tartness! ✯ Yield: 3 cups.

ROASTED CORN SALSA

8 large ears white corn, approximately 2 cups
1 large red bell pepper, small dice
½ cup purple onion, small dice
2 Serrano chile peppers, seeded & diced
4 tablespoons fresh cilantro, chopped
1 teaspoons fresh thyme, chopped
2 tablespoons rice wine vinegar
1 ½ teaspoons salt
2 tablespoons oil

Roast corn in skillet until it begins to brown and to caramelize natural sugars. ✯ In a separate container, mix remaining ingredients and add roasted corn. ✯ It is important to taste and correct the amount of fresh herbs and salt.

Eric

SALMON MARINADE

¼ cup brown sugar
¼ cup Jack Daniels
¼ cup spicy brown mustard (French's)
1 teaspoon chipotle puree
¼ cup vegetable oil
¼ cup water

Place salmon in marinade for 15 minutes to an hour before grilling. ✷
Add salt and pepper at the grill.

SHRIMP STOCK

¼ cup vegetable oil
¾ cup celery, diced
1 cup carrots, diced
3 cups onions, diced
1 tablespoon jalapeno, diced
½ cup tomato, diced
SHRIMP SHELLS from approximately 10 pounds of shrimp
¾ cup white wine
12 cups chicken stock
2 cups water
1 bay leaf
2 sprigs fresh thyme
½ cup Parsley, chopped

Place in a large pot and sauté for 3 minutes. Add the jalapeno,
tomato, and shrimp shells, sauté 3 minutes. Add wine, boil 1 minute.
Add remaining ingredients, simmer slowly for 20 minutes. (DO NOT
BOIL) Turn off heat and let sit for one hour. Strain. May be frozen.

TEXAS BBQ SAUCE

2 cups onions, small dice
2 cups celery, small dice
1 tablespoon garlic, minced
2 cups tomatoes
1 cup apple cider vinegar
1 cup dark brown sugar
1½ cups beef broth or stock
½ cup Worcestershire sauce
2 bay leaves
1 tablespoon black pepper, ground
1/2 teaspoon cayenne pepper (optional)
1 tablespoon cumin
1 tablespoon New Mexico red chile powder
1/2 teaspoon cinnamon, ground

Combine all ingredients and cook over medium heat until thickened. Stir often. Remove bay leaves. Place in food processor and puree.

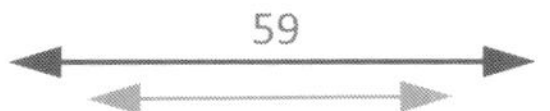

TOMATILLO-SERRANO CHILE SAUCE

1 ½ tablespoons olive oil
3 cups onions, diced
1 1/2 tablespoons garlic pureed
6 small or 3 large Serrano chilies
12 sprigs cilantro (separate leaves and stems)
1 1/2 pounds tomatillos, husked and washed
6 cups chicken stock
3 cups heavy cream
3 cups fresh spinach, packed well
Salt to taste

Chop cilantro stems fine and reserve. Reserve leaves. ✶ Heat oil in a large skillet. Sauté onions, three minutes. Add garlic and chilies and cook for one minute. ✶ Cook tomatillos in a separate dry skillet until lightly browned. Add tomatillos, cilantro stems, and chicken stock to sautéed onions in large pan. ✶ Bring to a boil and simmer 20 minutes. ✶ Add cream, reduce heat and cook 5 minutes. Remove Serrano chilies. Pour into processor adding cilantro leaves and spinach. Process until smooth. Taste for spice and add Serrano chilies one at a time. ✶ Taste for salt.

CAUTION: SERRANO CHILES MAY BE VERY HOT. I PUREE COOKED CHILES AND ADD TO SAUCE A TEASPOON AT A TIME, TASTING AFTER EACH ADDITION.

VINAIGRETTE

1 teaspoon garlic
1 teaspoon shallot
1 teaspoon salt
1 teaspoon black pepper, ground
1 tablespoon sugar
¾ cup rice wine vinegar
2 teaspoon balsamic vinegar
2 teaspoon Dijon mustard
1/4 teaspoon marjoram
1 ½ cup vegetable oil

Combine garlic and shallot in food processor. Add remaining ingredients, except oil. With the food processor running, very slowly pour oil in the processor to create an emulsion.

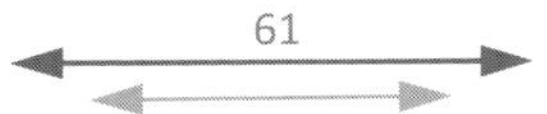

WHITE BEAN SALSA

One pound bacon cooked crisp and drained
(I dice the bacon before cooking and dice again after it has drained)
2 tablespoons bacon grease, reserved from cooking bacon
2 cups diced onions
1 ½ green onion, sliced thin
1 tablespoon garlic, pureed
1 tablespoon chipotle, pureed
2 cups chicken stock or broth
Juice of 1 lime
1 cup diced tomatoes

Using the same skillet, cook diced onions until soft and translucent. ✶ Add to the onions, green onion, garlic, chipotle and chicken stock or broth, bring to simmer. ✶ Stir in 6 cups canned white beans. *(If using dried follow package directions for cooking).* ✶ Stir in lime juice and diced tomatoes, bring to simmer ✶ Salt and Pepper to taste. Add more chicken stock for best consistency. ✶ Remove from heat. ✶ Refrigerate until ready to use.

Booty, Eric, Karen & Brandon

PERFECT PLATES
^^^^^^^^^^^^^^^^^^^^

There are times when we have all experienced that one great plate of food. I think I know why some plates of food are more outstanding than others. Presentation and taste are important, but perfection includes the following: *comfort* – soft food, even rich taste; *crunch* – something to bite into, a noise inside your head; *contrast* – a taste that cuts through the main flavors of the plate, a little something on the side.

The depth of flavor that I look for includes tastes in more than one place in your mouth. Like good wine, there are flavors on the tongue and in the back of the mouth, and flavors

that linger long after the food is swallowed, all the while imparting an intoxicating aroma!

First, Billy watched and asked questions. Then we cooked together and he asked more questions. We cooked, tasted, tested, made notes and talked ideas; our recipe books, (like our lives) have spills on their pages, (and a few tears), and more meaning for all the effort.

PORK TENDERLOIN FAJITAS
WITH APPLE RED CHILI CHUTNEY
& COLLARD GREENS

4 pounds pork tenderloin, trimmed of silver skin and fat
4 cups apple cider
¼ cup brown sugar
5 chili de arbol, (whole dried red chilies)
1½ tablespoons oil
3 cups onions, thinly sliced into rounds (about 2 large)
Salt and pepper to taste
Fried Collard Greens (page 67)
16 ten-inch flour tortillas, warmed and rolled
4 cups *Creamed Corn Salsa*, garnish (page 9)
4 cups *Georgia Grille Black Beans*, garnish (page 5)
½ cup *Apple Red Chili Chutney*, garnish (page 66)

Trim tenderloins well. Make a marinade of cider, brown sugar and chili de arbol. Put the tenderloins in a non-reactive dish. Pour marinade over them. Cover and refrigerate for 8 to 24 hours. ✪ Remove tenderloin from marinade. Strain marinade and reserve liquid. Pat tenderloin dry. Slice tenderloin into 24 equal portions, approximately 2-1/2 ounces each. Place each piece between plastic wrap and flatten with a mallet to ¼ inch thick. ✪ Heat the oil in a large, heavy bottom skillet. Add sliced onions and cook them over medium high heat about 20 minutes until soft and brown. Remove onions and keep warm. ✪ In the same skillet add pork a few pieces at a time. Do not overcrowd. Turn to brown each side, cooking about 2 minutes. Do not overcook. Pork should remain moist. ✪ Keep pork warm. Deglaze skillet with reserved marinade. Raise heat to

reduce marinade to one cup. Taste for salt and pepper. Return pork to skillet to reheat in sauce. ✪ Plate presentation: place 3 pieces of pork and top with some onions in a row across center of plate. Top the pork and onions with fried collard greens. Place two warmed and rolled tortillas on one side of pork. Make a strip of ½ cup of *Creamed Corn Salsa* and ½ cup of *Georgia Grille Black Beans* on the other side of pork. Place ½ cup of *Apple Red Chili Chutney* in a ramekin to the side. ✪ Yield: 8 servings.

APPLE RED CHILI CHUTNEY

3-1/2 cups tart red apples, peeled, seeds removed (about 4)
1 cup apple cider vinegar
1 cup dark brown sugar
1/2 cup water
1/2 cup granulated sugar
2 tablespoons red chili powder
1/2 teaspoon garlic, minced
1/4 cup walnuts, chopped
1/2 teaspoon dried marjoram

Rough chop the apples. Place apples, vinegar, brown sugar, water, granulated sugar, red chili powder and garlic in a large, heavy bottom, non-reactive pan. ✪ Cook over low heat, stirring often until water is absorbed and mixture has a very thick consistency. Remove from heat and stir in walnuts and marjoram. ✪ Store in glass container in refrigerator. ✪ Yield: approximately 4 cups.

FRIED COLLARD GREENS

1 pound fresh collard greens, trimmed, stems removed
oil for frying

Wash the collards well in several changes of water. Roll several leaves tightly into a cigar shape. Cut each "cigar" into 1/2-inch strips or chiffonade. ✪ Heat a very deep fryer to 360°. In small batches fry collard greens. They will bubble and spatter. When the spatter slows (15 seconds) remove and drain on lots of paper to absorb the oil. Serve immediately or keep crisp. ✪ Yield: 2 loose cups.

Mark

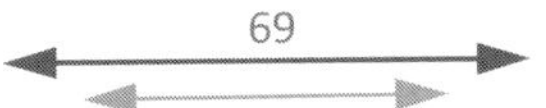

GRILLED SALMON QUESADILLA
WITH CHIPOTLE CREAM SAUCE
& SQUASH SALSA

*Once you gather all the ingredients, this is a relatively easy,
very special plate of food to serve.*

6 eight-inch flour tortillas
3/4 cup *Chipotle Cream Sauce* (page 70, note)
3 tablespoons *Serrano Chili Oil* divided, (page 23)
6 cups spinach leaves, well rinsed, with some of the water still on
the leaves
3 cups warmed *Georgia Grille Black Beans* (page 5)
3 pounds salmon fillet, boneless and skinless
   (3/4 to 1 inch thick)
6 cups *Squash Salsa* (page 71)
Twigs garnish (page 16)

Spread 2 tablespoons *Chipotle Cream Sauce* on a flour tortilla. Place
the tortilla in a large non-stick skillet over medium heat, sauce side
up. Cook to soften tortilla and warm the cream sauce, about 2
minutes. Repeat with remaining tortillas. (We do this on a large flat
griddle at the restaurant). ✪ Place tortillas in single layer on a large
baking sheet and cover with foil. Keep warm in a very low oven,
125° to 150°. ✪ In the same skillet over medium heat, sprinkle a
tablespoon of *Serrano Chili Oil*. Add spinach. Toss until the sizzle
subsides and divide spinach equally on tortillas. Add 1/2 cup of the
warmed black beans to each tortilla. ✪ Slice salmon fillets into 18
pieces. There will be three slices per quesadilla. In a large skillet,
heat remaining *Serrano Chili Oil* and cook salmon fillets 6 to 9

minutes, turning once. Place cooked salmon on top of the spinach, dividing it into three portions per tortilla. You can grill the salmon rather than sautéing if you prefer. ✪ Top each with 1 cup *Squash Salsa*. Garnish with *Twigs*. ✪ Yield: 6 entrees.

> NOTES TO BILLY:
> *How to Soften Flour Tortillas*
> *Method #1: warm flour tortillas on grill, or under broiler just until soft. Roll and keep warm.*
> *Method #2: place tortillas in hot chicken stock for ten seconds, remove and fill immediately.*
> *Method #3: wrap tortillas in a damp terry cloth towel and warm in a 200 degree oven.*

CHIPOTLE CREAM SAUCE

1 cup heavy cream
1 tablespoon canned Chipotle in
   Adobe sauce, pureed (see note)
1 small garlic clove, pureed
   (about 1/2 teaspoon)
1 cup sour cream
1/8 teaspoon white pepper
3/4 teaspoon salt

> NOTES TO BILLY:
> *I puree the entire contents of a can of Chipotle in Adobe sauce, then store it in a glass jar in the refrigerator. I measure out what I need.*

Combine cream, chipotle pepper and some of the adobe sauce and garlic in pan over medium heat and reduce by one third. ✪ Remove from heat and stir in sour cream, white pepper and salt. ✪ This sauce can be stored in the refrigerator for two days. Bring it back to room temperature, i.e., spreadable consistency, for use with flour tortillas, or reheat it very slowly over low heat. Do not boil or the sauce will separate. ✪ Yield: six 1/4-cup servings; 1-1/2 cups total.

SQUASH SALSA

This is a visually stunning salsa. The trick is to use only the skin and 1/4 inch of the flesh of the zucchini and squash to get the wonderful dark colors.

1 large zucchini, julienne skin and only 1/4 inch flesh (about 1 cup)
2 yellow squash, julienne skin and 1/4 inch flesh (about 1 cup)
1 carrot, julienned (about 1 cup)
1/4 cup diced purple onion, rinsed in cold water
1/2 cup rice vinegar
2 tablespoons olive oil
1 tablespoon lemon juice
2 teaspoons pickled jalapeño puree (see note page 30)
1-1/2 teaspoons sugar
1 garlic clove, minced
3/4 teaspoon salt
1 pinch leaf marjoram

Cut julienne sticks of zucchini, yellow squash and carrots into small dice. Add the rinsed onions. ✪ Mix together the vinegar, olive oil, lemon juice, jalapeño puree, sugar, garlic clove, salt and marjoram. Pour over vegetables. Toss. Check for salt. ✪ Yield: six 1/2-cup servings; 2-1/2 cups total.

SHRIMP AND SCALLOPS
WITH TOMATO, RED PEPPER
AND GARLIC SAUCE AND FRIED GRIT CAKES

Be careful not to overcook the shrimp and scallops in this recipe.

18 large shrimp, peeled and de-veined
18 large sea scallops
2 tablespoons *Black Pepper Spice Rub*
1 tablespoon *Serrano Chili Oil* (page 23)
6 cups *Tomato Red Pepper and Garlic Sauce* (page 73)
1/4 cup dry white wine
1/2 cup *Roasted Garlic Butter* (page 10)
Fried Grits (page 73), garnish
Twigs garnish (page 16)

Dust shrimp and scallops with *Black Pepper Spice Rub*. Heat a large sauté pan over medium heat, add chili oil. When oil is hot, add shrimp and scallops. Cook until shrimp turns barely pink, about 2 minutes, stirring and turning to cook evenly. ✪ Stir in 6 cups *Tomato Red Pepper and Garlic Sauce*. Bring to a boil, reduce heat and add white wine. Remove from heat and stir in *Roasted Garlic Butter*. ✪ Divide among six plates. Garnish with fried grits and *Twigs*. ✪ Yield: 6 entrée servings; 12 appetizer servings.

BLACK PEPPER SPICE RUB

1/3 cup black pepper
1/3 cup garlic powder
1/3 cup paprika
1/4 cup salt
1/2 teaspoon cayenne

Mix all together. Store in an air tight jar. ✪ Yield: 1-1/4 cups.

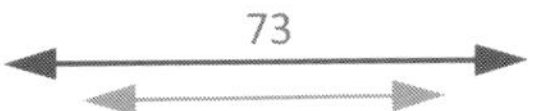

TOMATO, RED PEPPER
AND GARLIC SAUCE

Use for shrimp and scallops, pasta or as the base for Veracruz Sauce.

2 28-ounce cans of good quality tomatoes, drained and diced
    (about 4 cups)
1 large tomato, seeded and diced (about 1 cup)
2 cups green onions, green and white parts, diced (about 9)
2 large red bell peppers, roasted, peeled, seeded, diced,
    (about 2 cups, see *Smoking and Roasting*, page 29)
1 medium onion, diced
2 tablespoons garlic cloves, minced (about 2 large)
2 tablespoons salt

Combine all ingredients and store in refrigerator in airtight container.
✪ Yield: 6 cups.

FRIED GRIT CAKES

2 cups Venezuela white corn flour (available in Hispanic markets)
(Note: If you are unable to find corn flour, you can substitute
white grits.)
2 teaspoons salt
4 ounces Monterey Jack cheese, grated (about 1 cup)
3 cups warm water
Oil for frying

Combine corn flour and salt in a mixer. Stir in cheese. Pour in water
and blend. ✪ Let grits set until firm. Shape with hands into flat
disks about 2 inches across. ✪ Heat vegetable oil to 360°. Drop
grits disks into hot oil a few at a time and fry until golden brown. ✪
Yield: eight 2-cake servings; 16 grits cakes total.

Shine

HICKORY GRILLED TENDERLOIN
WITH BLACK BEANS, FRIED ONION RINGS
AND RIPE TOMATO RELISH

*Splurge on this dish by purchasing prime quality fillets
for an out-of-this world treat.*

6 eight-ounce beef tenderloin fillets
1-1/2 teaspoons *Black Pepper Spice Rub* (page 72)
6 cups *Georgia Grille Black Beans* (page 5)
3 cups *Ripe Tomato Relish* (page 76)
Fried Onion Rings (page 77)

Bring fillets to room temperature. Pat dry. Dust each side of fillet
with *Black Pepper Spice Rub* no more than 5 minutes before grilling,
otherwise the salt draws the juices from the steak, making it tough and
dry. ✪ For maximum flavor, grill over hickory 7 to 8 minutes,
turning once. You can cook the fillets on a gas grill, charcoal, under a
broiler or in a sauté pan, but for the very best flavor, cook over a
hickory wood fire. ✪ Let the fillets rest five minutes, covered, before
serving. Any juice that has accumulated should be drizzled over the
fillet. ✪ Plate presentation: place the fillet on the plate. Spoon 1
cup of black beans on one side and a 1/2 cup of *Ripe Tomato Relish*
on the other side. Mound a handful of *Fried Onion Rings* on top of
each fillet. ✪ Yield: 6 entrees.

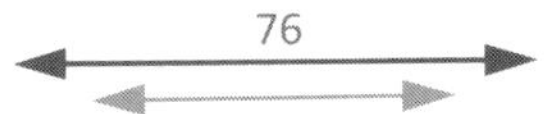

RIPE TOMATO RELISH

Serve with grilled meats, seafood, or vegetables.

8 cups ripe tomatoes, seeded and chopped (about 6 large)
3/4 teaspoon salt
1-3/4 cups sugar
1-1/2 cups white vinegar
1-1/2 tablespoons garlic, pureed, (about 4 large cloves)
1/2 cup green bell pepper, diced, (about 1/2 pepper)
1/2 cup red bell pepper, diced, (about ½)
2 jalapeños, sliced
1 teaspoon allspice
1 teaspoon cinnamon
1 teaspoon ground cloves
1 teaspoon nutmeg

Coarsely chop tomatoes and mix with salt. Set in a colander to drain while preparing the rest of the ingredients. ✪ Combine all ingredients, including drained tomatoes, in a large pot. Bring to a boil, reduce heat and simmer to reduce liquid by one-third. Store in refrigerator. ✪ Yield: approximately 10 cups. ✪ *Note*: If you want to preserve a large quantity, you can follow Ball Jar or other manufacturers' instructions for canning or preserving without refrigeration.

FRIED ONION RINGS

Serve with grilled meats, seafood, or vegetables.

3 Medium to large onions
4 Cups self rising flour or more as needed
Oil for frying
Salt

Peel onions. Slice into 1/4 inch rings. (Use a mandolin, if you have one, to keep the onions uniform and thin.) Separate the rings and put them in a large bowl of cold water. ✪ Heat the oil to 360° for frying. Taking a large handful of onion rings, shake off excess water and toss into self rising flour mixed with salt to taste. Shake off excess flour and drop in hot oil. ✪ Fry until lightly golden. Continue with additional onions until all are fried. Drain well on paper towels. Taste and sprinkle with additional salt, if needed. ✪ Yield: 6 servings as accompaniment to entrée; 1 large plateful as an appetizer for several people.

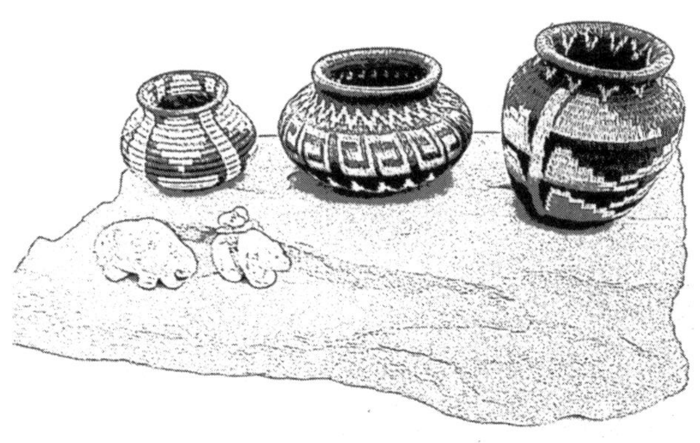

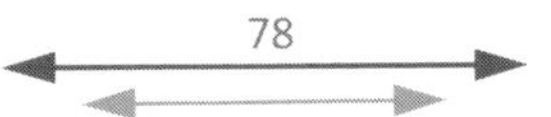

VEGETABLE BURRITO
WITH SMOKED TOMATO DRIZZLE

1 cup onion, diced (about 1 medium)
2 garlic cloves, pureed, through a garlic press (about 1 tablespoon)
1 tablespoon *Pickled Jalapeño Puree* (see note page 41)
2 tablespoons oil
4 ounces mushrooms, medium dice, (about 1-1/2 cups)
1 cup zucchini, medium dice, (about 1)
1 cup yellow squash, medium dice, (about 2)
1/2 cup carrots, shredded (about 1)
1 cup of leaf spinach, packed
1 medium tomato, seeded and diced, (about 1/2 cup)
1/2 cup dry white wine
1/2 cup Sierra cheese, grated (Monterey Jack cheese can be substituted)
1/2 cup fresh herbs, chopped, such as flat leaf parsley, thyme, marjoram, oregano
6 ten-inch whole wheat flour tortillas
6 ounces Monterey Jack cheese, grated
1-1/2 cups *Smoked Tomato Drizzle* (page 79)
1/4 cup fresh cilantro leaves, garnish
6 tablespoons roasted pumpkin seeds, (see *Notes to Billy*), garnish (raw pumpkin seeds are available at health food stores)

Sauté the onions, garlic and jalapeño in oil in an extra large skillet or a Dutch oven until onions begin to brown. Stir in mushrooms and sauté for two minutes. Stir in zucchini, yellow squash and carrots and cook for two minutes. ✪ Add spinach and cook for one minute. Add

tomatoes and wine, and cook for two minutes, stirring well. ✪ Stir in Sierra cheese and remove from heat. Add fresh chopped herbs and parsley. Check the salt and pepper level; the cheese is fairly salty so you may not need any. ✪ Soften tortillas (page 40) and fill them with the vegetable mixture. Roll into burrito and sprinkle with the Monterey Jack cheese. Spoon several spoonfuls of the *Smoked Tomato Drizzle* over the burrito. Serve immediately or reheat in 350° oven. Garnish with fresh cilantro leaves and roasted pumpkin seeds. ✪ Yield: six 10-inch Burritos or twelve 6-inch burritos.

> *Notes to Billy:*
> *To Roast Pumpkin Seeds*
> *Heat a well seasoned black iron skillet over medium heat, add 6 tablespoons of Pumpkin Seeds and stir until the seeds are toasted. Sprinkle the seeds lightly with salt. If a black iron skillet is not available, use a heavy skillet and spray with cooking spray.*

SMOKED TOMATO DRIZZLE

This sauce is an example of how rich and unusual a dish can be using a different technique on one of the ingredients. This breakthrough occurred as a result of my "discovery" of smoking.

6 Roma tomatoes, hickory smoked, then peeled
3 medium tomatoes, pureed, (about 1 cup)
   or 1 cup canned tomato puree
1 tablespoon olive oil
pinch of salt

Puree smoked Roma tomatoes. Strain both the smoked and the un-smoked tomato to remove their seeds. Combine the strained purees and simmer over low heat with the olive oil and salt to taste. Cook for 12 minutes until slightly thickened. ✪ Yield: four 1/2-cup servings.

Brandon

NEW PLATES

In a professional kitchen for more years of my life than not, I discovered food combinations dance in my head. Some combinations were winners and others discarded quickly. Some new plates became customer favorites and moved to a permanent spot on the menu. We adopted the idea of weeknight specials so as not to overload the kitchen staff and now customers come for their favorite. We use Friday and Saturday for "special" specials.

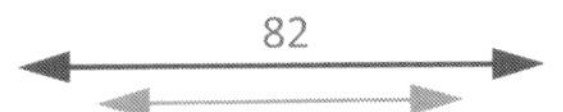

CATFISH

6 eight ounce portions of catfish filet, cut in half.
2 cups buttermilk to 1 cup Dijon mustard.
Flour, seasoned (page 5)
     1 cup flour
     1 teaspoon kosher salt
     ½ teaspoon black pepper

Dredge catfish in buttermilk mustard mixture then in flour. Deep fry until golden brown. See *Frying* below.

Plate Presentation:
Cover plate with *Tomatillo Serrano Chile Sauce* (page 59). ✶ Place Catfish over sauce. ✶ Top Catfish with *Jalapeno Cole Slaw* (page 83)

FRYING

I believe that people eat fried foods at restaurants because it is very difficult to do at home. It takes experience and the proper equipment to have success at frying your favorite foods. My best advice is to follow instructions from a technical source for home cooks, know your equipment well and do not be too ambitious.   Good luck!

JALAPENO COLE SLAW

Slaw:

    4 cups shredded raw cabbage
    ½ cup julienne carrots
    ½ cup purple cabbage shredded

Dressing:

    2 cups mayonnaise
    1-1/2 tablespoons Jalapeno, puree
    ¼ cup lemon juice
    ¼ cup rice wine vinegar
    3 tablespoons sugar

Pour dressing over slaw until desired consistency.

CRAYFISH ENCHILADA

Filling:

    ½ cup clarified butter
    1 1/3 cups green onions, finely chopped
    4# Louisiana frozen crayfish tails (including liquid)
    1 teaspoon salt
    1 teaspoon white pepper
    1 teaspoon cayenne
    1 teaspoon oregano
    2 cups Monterey Jack cheese, shredded

Sauté green onions in butter. Mix seasoning in large bowl. Toss with crayfish. Stir into green onion and heat through. ✶ Yield: approximately 8 cups. ✶ Keep refrigerated until ready to serve.

Sauce:

    1 tablespoon clarified butter
    2 teaspoons salt
    1 teaspoon white pepper
    ½ teaspoon oregano
    1 teaspoon garlic
    1 teaspoon cayenne
    2 cups green chile (diced, roasted)
    6 cups chicken stock
    2 cups heavy cream
    4 cups Monterey Jack cheese

Melt butter in heavy pot. Stir in salt, white pepper, oregano, garlic and cayenne. Add green chiles and chicken stock. Bring to boil. Stir in heavy cream and reduce to half. Remove from heat. Stir in Monterey Jack cheese and stir well. DO NOT BOIL ✶ Makes approximately 8 cups ✶ Keep refrigerated until ready to serve.

24 six inch blue corn tortillas

To serve: Place blue corn tortilla on plate. Ladle 2 oz sauce and ¼ cup crayfish mixture. Repeat. Top with the third tortilla, sauce and crayfish. Additionally top with ¼ cup Monterey jack cheese. Place under broiler to melt cheese. ✶ Serves 8

FISH TACOS

Tilapia filets cut in one inch pieces (6-8 oz per serving)
2 cups buttermilk
1 cup Dijon mustard
flour, seasoned with salt and pepper

Toss tilapia in buttermilk mustard mixture then in flour. Fry until golden brown. See *Frying* (page 82)
Soften two 6" flour tortilla over heat. Spread with *Chipotle Cream Sauce* (page 70) Fill with fried tilapia and *Jalapeno Cole Slaw* (page 83) Add a side of jalapeños

Pete

LAMB TENDERLOIN QUESADILLA

Lamb tenderloins, approximately 6 ounces per person
½ cup olive oil
1 tablespoon fresh rosemary
1 tablespoon mustard
1 tablespoon Worcestershire sauce

Combine all ingredients to make a loose paste. Spread over all the meat. Place meat in a plastic bag and refrigerate overnight. ✶ Remove and slice meat across the grain into ¼ inch slices. Place between sheets of plastic and pound thin. ✶ Lightly oil a skillet (I use a black iron skillet) and place over medium high heat. Sear each piece quickly. Do not over cook. Do not crowd the skillet. Remove and keep warm.

Per serving:
    Flour tortilla
    Chipotle Cream Sauce (page 70)
    Fresh baby spinach
    White Bean Salsa (page 61)
    Fresh arugula
    Vinaigrette (page 60)
    Habanera Mint Sauce (page 51)
    Sprig of fresh watercress
    Diced tomato

Crisp the flour tortilla in the oven, skillet or flat grill. ✶ Spread with *Chipotle Cream Sauce*. Place on dinner plate and top with spinach and white bean salsa (warm). ✶ Toss arugula lightly in vinaigrette and place on top. Place lamb slices over the arugula. With a squeeze bottle make ribbons of *Habanera Mint Sauce* across the top. ✶ Garnish with a sprig of fresh watercress and diced tomato.

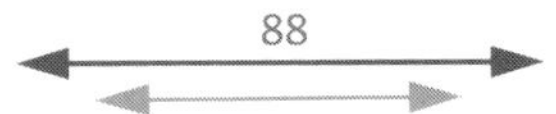

NAVAJO TACO

2 tablespoons oil
2 cups onions, small dice
5 pounds beef, ground
2 pounds chorizo

Sauté the onions until translucent. Stir in ground beef and chorizo, breaking apart and cooking until well browned. Stir in one cup of water and cook over low heat until tender, approximately one hour.

To Serve: Place one taco on a dinner plate and top with ½ cup Monterey jack cheese. Place under broiler to melt the cheese. Spoon 1 ½ cups meat over cheese, pour ½ cup *Green Chile Sauce* (page 17) over the meat. Top with shredded lettuce, 2 tablespoons *Fresh Tomato Salsa* (page 11) and 1 tablespoon sour cream.

INDIAN FRY BREAD

3 cups flour
½ cup non-fat dry milk
1 tablespoon baking powder
1 tablespoon salt
3 tablespoon Crisco
1 ¼ cup warm water

Combine flour, dry milk, baking powder and salt in heavy mixer bowl. Add Crisco and cut into dry ingredients in the mixing bowl at low speed. Gradually add water, stir until mixture becomes a dough ball. Roll into equal portions, about 12. Flatten each ball with your hands a stretch into a circle. Puncture a small hole in the middle. ✻ Fry in hot oil for tacos until the dough puffs up and turn light brown. Drain on paper towels.

SHRIMP ENCHILADA

Sauce:

    8 tablespoons shallots, minced
    4 tablespoons garlic, minced
    4 tablespoons jalapeño, minced
    12 cups chicken stock
    2 quarts heavy cream
    4 smoked red bell peppers, small dice
    4 cups tomatoes, small dice
    4 tablespoons cilantro, chopped
    1 teaspoon marjoram
    juice of 2 limes
    6 cups Monterey Jack cheese

    36 large shrimp
    12 6" flour tortillas
    Fresh Tomato Salsa, garnish (page 11)

Sweat shallots, garlic and jalapeños in heavy pan. Add chicken stock and reduce by ½. Add cream and slowly reduce by ½. Stir in remaining ingredients except for cheese and shrimp. Reduce to correct consistency. ✴ For twelve enchiladas (six servings): Plunge the shrimp into boiling salted water. Dice and stir in small amount of sauce. Divide the shrimp between the twelve 6" inch flour tortillas. Place side by side on a baking dish, seam side down and cover with sauce just to the edges. Top with shredded Monterey Jack cheese. Place in 350 degree oven and bake 12-15 minutes until lightly browned on the edges and hot in the center. ✴ Top with *Fresh Tomato Salsa*. (page 11)

This recipe came about after a very great rise in the price of lobster and for our Lobster Enchilada. We use the same sauce for the shrimp and it has become a favorite on the menu!

Erin & Beth

GREEN CHILE CHEESE QUICHE

1 unbaked pie shell
9 ounces cheddar or Monterey Jack cheese
6 tablespoons *Green Chile Sauce* (page 17)
5 eggs
2 tablespoons grated parmesan
¾ cup whipping cream

Heat oven to 400 degrees. ✶ (*I use Hefty EZ foil 8 inch pans*) Fill unbaked shell with cheeses and green chile. Lightly whip the eggs and add cream. ✶ Pour over cheese using fork to separate the cheeses and let the cream mix with the filling. ✶ Bake at 400 degrees for 15 minutes. Reduce heat to 350 degrees for 15 minutes. Lightly cover with foil and continue to bake until lightly browned and somewhat firm in the middle.

Booty

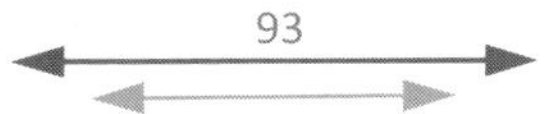

DAN'S MARGERITA

*Dan Rather is a long time friend and customer at Georgia Grille. He suggested
we needed a "Mexican Margarita" on the menu and gave me this recipe.*

2 parts Silver Tequila
1 part Triple Sec
Juice of one lime

Pour into shaker filled with ice. Shake well. Pour over one ice filled
Margarita glass rimmed with salt. Garnish with lime wedge.

Thanks Dan!

Karen

SOMETHING SWEET

Everyone is soft and sweet, kind and gentle when we start talking desserts. One lick off the end of your finger can bring a smile even when there is so much left to do and not enough time to get ready. "Getting ready" are the key words in the restaurant business, and they are the secret to fantastic desserts. There is always a deadline that does not allow for long conversation and experimentation. Consider the process: there must be

product availability, Knowledgeable staff and proper

equipment, as well as time and space. Every menu choice must be capable of being produced, along with everything else that is on the menu, and they all must appear at just the right moment at the customer's table. It's 50% magic, of course. Everyone who cooks at Georgia Grille gets to make desserts. . . it makes us all smile. I'll have chocolate, thank you.

Booty, Eric & Brandon

BANANA CHEESECAKE FLAUTA

2 8 ounce packages cream cheese

1 cup sugar

3 eggs

3 tablespoons fresh squeezed lemon juice

1 ½ teaspoon vanilla extract

1/4 teaspoon salt

2 cup sour cream

1 cup mashed ripe banana

Butter a "9" baking pan. ✶ Preheat the oven to 350 degrees. ✶ In a large mixing bowl, beat the cream cheese and sugar until very smooth about 3 minutes. Add the eggs one at a time, beating after each addition, scraping down the sides, until smooth. Add in the vanilla and salt and beat until incorporated. Beat in sour cream just until blended. ✶ Mix lemon juice and mashed bananas together and then add to cream cheese mixture. Pour the batter into the prepared pan. Set the pan in the larger pan and surround it with 1 inch of very hot water. ✶ Bake 45 minutes. ✶ Turn off the oven without opening the door and let cake cool for one hour. ✶ Remove to rack and cool to room temperature. ✶ Refrigerate overnight. ✶ Place about 3/4 cup of cheesecake in a 6"-10" whole wheat tortilla and secure with toothpick. ✶ Fry in hot oil. ✶ Garnish with *Vanilla Pouring Sauce* (page 106), strawberries or blueberries and whipped cream.

BLACKBERRY PEACH COBBLER

This is hands-on cooking. You only need a measuring cup,
spoon, baking dish, and a bowl to make the crust.

2-1/2 cups all-purpose flour
1/2 teaspoon baking soda
1/2 teaspoon salt
4 ounces Crisco
3/4 cup milk
1 twenty-ounce package frozen peaches, partially thawed (about
2-1/2 cups)
1 twelve-ounce package frozen blackberries, partially thawed
(about 1-1/2 cups)
1/2 cup sugar
2 ounces butter

Preheat oven to 400°. ✪ In large bowl, combine flour, baking soda,
salt and Crisco. Cut in the Crisco with your hands, until mixture
resembles large, coarse grains. ✪ Add the milk to the flour mixture.
Stir to combine. Turn out on table and gently pat into rectangle to fit
a 3-quart rectangular casserole. ✪ Mix partially thawed fruit in 3-
quart rectangular casserole. Cover with pastry. Sprinkle with sugar
and dot with butter. Bake at 400° for 25 to 30 minutes. ✪ Yield: 8
servings.

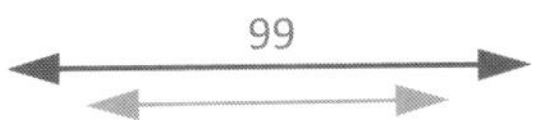

BREAD PUDDING

3 eggs, large
1 ¼ cups sugar
1 ½ teaspoons vanilla extract
1 teaspoon ground cinnamon
¼ cup butter, melted
2 cups milk
½ cup walnuts, chopped
5 cups *Honey Whole Wheat Bread* (page 18), diced

Preheat oven to 350 degrees. Butter a loaf pan. ✷ Mix together all ingredients except bread. ✷ Add bread and soak for about 45 minutes. ✷ Pour into a loaf pan. ✷ Bake for 45 minutes at 350 degrees. ✷ Turn heat up to 425 degrees for 15 minutes.

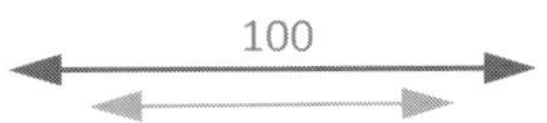

David

Ron

Tyrone

COCOA MOCHA ICE CREAM PIE

Crust:
 3 cups pecans, finely chopped
 5 tablespoons butter, softened
 2 teaspoons vanilla or dark rum
 ¼ cup brown sugar
 1 cup coconut, toasted

Combine all ingredients, divide in half and press into two eight or nine inch pie pans. ✶ Freeze until ready to fill.

Filling: Layer the following over the crust. (Freeze after each layer)
 2 cups dark chocolate ice cream
 2 cups vanilla ice cream
 1 cup coffee ice cream
 ½ cup dark chocolate chunks

Spread chocolate ice cream layer over the crust. Freeze.
Spread vanilla ice cream over the chocolate and freeze.
Slightly soften the coffee ice cream and stir in chocolate chunks.
Spread over the top. Freeze.

To serve: Cut into six wedges. Top with lightly sweetened whipped cream and a maraschino cherry. ✶ Sprinkle with dark chocolate pieces, chopped. And drizzle with *Ganache* (page 102)

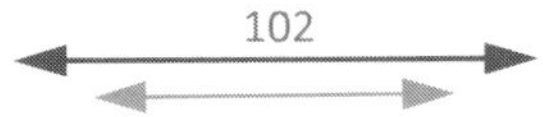

GANACHE

16 oz semi sweet chocolate
4-6 oz heavy cream, heated
2 teaspoons vanilla

In food processor, process chocolate. With processor running pour in hot cream and continue until the chocolate is smooth. Add vanilla.

GLAZED BLUEBERRY CAKE
with Vanilla Pouring Cream

1/3 cup sugar
¼ cup water
1 tablespoon fresh lemon juice
1 teaspoon cornstarch
3 cups blueberries (washed and stems removed)

Stir together 1/3 cup sugar with water, lemon juice and cornstarch in a small saucepan add blueberries. Bring to a simmer, stirring for three minutes. Remove from heat.

1 cup flour
1 ¾ teaspoons baking powder
1 teaspoon salt
½ cup sugar
1 large egg
½ cup milk
½ cup butter, melted
1 teaspoon vanilla

Butter a 9" pan and sprinkle with sugar. Preheat oven to 375 degrees. ✻ Whisk together flour, baking powder, salt and sugar. In a separate bowl whisk together egg, milk, melted butter and vanilla. Stir into flour mixture until just combined. Spoon batter into prepared pan and then pour blueberry mixture over the top. Do not stir. ✻

Holiday version: Substitute cranberries for blueberries.

GRAN MARNIER FLAN
WITH TOASTED HAZELNUT CRUMBS AND FRESH FRUIT

An easy, do-ahead holiday dessert.

1/2 cup sugar (for caramel)
2 cups milk
3 eggs
2 egg yolks
1/2 cup sugar
1 tablespoon Gran Marnier
1/2 teaspoon vanilla
1 cup toasted hazelnuts, chopped (walnuts or pecans can be substituted)
1 cup sliced strawberries or whole raspberries or blueberries, etc.

Preheat oven to 350°. Caramelize sugar in skillet, being careful not to burn. Pour hot sugar into six 6-ounce custard cups rotating to cover bottom of cups with the caramel. ✪ Scald milk by bringing it to a boil. Whisk eggs and egg yolks with 1/2 cup sugar. Stir in hot milk, Gran Marnier and vanilla. Whisk well to dissolve sugar. Pour mixture into cup until 3/4 full. ✪ Place cups in roasting pan filled with 1/2 inch hot water. Bake in 350° oven for 25 to 30 minutes. Don't cook too long. If the custard is overcooked, it will be too hard, if undercooked, too runny. When you insert a knife blade into the custard, it should come out clean, but the custard should not be hard. Cool and then refrigerate. ✪ Toast hazelnuts in a skillet over medium heat or in the oven until golden brown and aromatic. Chop finely. ✪ At serving time, run a knife around the edge of the custard cups. Put a plate upside down on top of the custard cup. Flip the plate and cup simultaneously to invert the custard cup and free the custard for serving on the plate. Sprinkle flans with the nuts and fruit. ✪ Yield: 6 individual servings.

TRIPLE CHOCOLATE MOUSSE

Chocolate mousse recipes are all very similar. I decided to stir the "crust" and the "topping" into the mousse to make serving it easier.

2 ounces bittersweet chocolate, melted for chocolate sheets
12 ounces bittersweet chocolate
1/2 cup strong hot coffee
1/2 cup sugar
4 *eggs*, separated (use pasteurized eggs if desired)
1 tablespoon dark rum
pinch salt
1/4 teaspoon cream of tartar
3/4 cup sugar
3 cups heavy whipping cream
1/2 package chocolate wafers *(Note: Nabisco Famous Chocolate Wafers are the best, but hard to find. When I do find them, I hoard and freeze them. However, other chocolate wafers can be used.)*
1/2 cup whipped cream, garnish optional
1/2 cup warmed fudge sauce, garnish optional

Melt 2 ounces chocolate and spread on sheet pan spayed with Pam. Chill and scrape off into sheets. Break up sheets into large pieces. Reserve. ✪ Process chocolate in food processor until fine granules. While machine is running, add 1/2 cup sugar to chocolate and pour in hot coffee. Add egg yolks, one at a time and process until smooth. Add rum. ✪ In a large bowl, beat the egg whites and salt with a mixer until foamy. Add cream of tartar and whip until peaks begin to form. Gradually add 3/4 cup sugar. Beat until moderately stiff. ✪ In another bowl, whip the cream until soft peaks form. Fold the whipped cream into chocolate mixture. The mixture is very thick and you will have streaks of chocolate and cream. Fold in the *egg* white/

sugar mixture, then fold in the chocolate wafers and the broken chocolate sheets. Pour into serving container and freeze. ✪ Remove from freezer 1 hour before serving. Garnish with whipped cream and hot fudge sauce. ✪ Yield: 8 generous servings.

VANILLA POURING CREAM

2 cups milk
¾ cup sugar
4 whole eggs
2 egg yolks
1 teaspoon vanilla
2 tablespoons butter (cold)

Combine sugar and milk in a heavy bottomed pan. Heat to simmer. Turn down the heat very low (or even off)! Whisk eggs in a small bowl. Stir in a small amount of the heated milk/sugar to the eggs to warm them. Repeat. (If the eggs curdle because the heat is too high you will have to start over) Slowly stir a small amount of eggs at a time into the warm milk and sugar mixture and continue stirring the heat very low. The mixture will thicken slightly, coating the back of a spoon. Remove from heat. ✶ At this point I strain the mixture into a chilled bowl to stop the cooking. Stir in vanilla and butter. ✶ Yield: approximately 2 ½ cups.

Karen

INDEX

INDEX